BUYING FROM
UNCLE SAM

VOLUME I

by
Carol M. Bright
&
William R. Winston

Published by
Clarendon House

Acknowledgments

We would like to thank several people around the country for their help in researching and compiling this directory. Our thanks to Dianne Brown for the months you devoted to this project. Deep appreciation to Mary Ellen for all the long distance phone calls and for coordinating everyone and everything. Many thanks to John Baylies and Lee Olsen for your time and expertise. We are grateful to Jeffrey G. Armstrong for your tremendous research work and the surplus auction material you provided. Thanks also to Joanne H. for the hours and hours of help and assistance.

This book would also not be possible without the help of the many government agencies and offices around the country who were so helpful and courteous. Their contributions, time, patience and information are gratefully acknowledged and very much appreciated.

Finally, many thanks to our families who put up with countless days and nights of TV dinners and Happy Meals so that we could continue working. We couldn't have done it without your help.

A Note From The Publisher

We have made every effort to achieve total accuracy of all the information we have presented. However, we cannot be held responsible for any errors that have inadvertently been made, or for changes in any of the information since we went to press.

Also, please note that we are not affiliated with any of the business entities or personnel referred to in this work. Neither are we able to offer legal, technical or financial advice, and urge the reader to <u>always</u> consult with his or her professional advisor before proceeding.

Table of Contents

Auction Summary Table

Use this table as a guide to the types of auctions referred to in this book.

AUCTION TYPE:	TYPES OF PROPERTY*:	PAGE NUMBERS:
BATF	V	166
BUREAU OF LAND MGMT.	RE	103,166-170
CITY POLICE	B,CAM,C,E,J,PP,S,V	17-19
COUNTY SHERIFF	A,C,E,J,O,PP,RE,V	37-45
CUSTOMS SERVICE, U.S.	A,B,C,E,J,LV,P,PP,RE,S,V	3,12,93,97-101,183
DEA - DRUG ENF. AGENCY	A,B,C,E,J,LV,P,PP,RE,S,V	3,53
DOA - DEPT OF AGRICULT.	C,O,V	175-176
DoD - DEPT OF DEFENSE	B,C,CAM,E,O,P,PP,V	3,121-133,183
DRMO / DRMS	B,C,CAM,E,O,P,PP,V	11,12,121-133
FDIC	A,C,E,J,O,PP,RE	171-175
GSA - GEN. SERV. ADMIN.	B,C,E,O,P,PP,RE,V	11,12,54,103-119,166,175,184
IRS - INT. REVENUE SERV.	A,B,C,E,J,LV,O,P,PP,RE,S,V	91-96,103,105
MARSHALS, CITY/COUNTY	A,C,CAM,E,J,LV,O,PP,S,V	37-45
MARSHALS SERVICE, U.S.	A,B,C,E,J,LV,O,P,PP,RE,S,V	1,53-63,104,186
POSTAL SERVICE, U.S.	C,J,O,PP,V	47-51
SBA - SM. BUSINESS ADMIN	C,E,J,O,PP,RE,S,V	135-146
STATE SURPLUS	B,C,CAM,E,LV,O,PP,V	65-89
TVA - TENN VALLEY AUTH.	C,E,O,PP,RE,V	165-166

*PROPERTY DESCRIPTIONS:
A = ANTIQUES, COLLECTIBLES, ARTWORK
B = BOATS, VESSELS
C = COMPUTER EQUIPMENT
CAM = CAMERAS, VIDEO EQUIPMENT
E = ELECTRONIC EQUIPMENT
J = JEWELRY, COINS
LV = LUXURY VEHICLES
P = PLANES, AIRCRAFT

PP = PERSONAL PROPERTY
RE = REAL ESTATE
S = STEREO EQUIPMENT
V = VEHICLES (CARS, TRUCKS, 4-WHEEL DRIVES, MOTOR-CYCLES, ETC.)

Chapter 1:
Introduction

> "There's really nothing quite like it. When I went to my first auction, it was a weekend lark. Now I own a business where both I and my son make a living reselling the items we buy at auctions. I even bought the building where I do my business and the trucks I haul in at an auction!"
>
> C. Kearny

Each year well over $300 billion of items are auctioned off across the United States. In 1993 alone, the dollar value of residential, commercial, and agricultural real estate sold through auctions hit an all-time high of $38.5 billion. Every year the U.S. Marshals Service auctions more than 6,000 items of forfeited property (cars, boats, aircraft, jewelry, collectibles, art) for a gross sales price of over $195 million!

These auctions vary in size and scope, but one element remains true regardless of who is holding the auction, where it is being held, or even when it occurs. Cars are sold at fantastic prices. Now, with the help of this book, you are going to know exactly how to get your next car at a bargain price way below wholesale.

How would you like to be able to save literally several thousands of dollars each year on cars, boats, planes, houses and other items you want to purchase? Not only do these incredible auctions provide you with a very real opportunity to save yourself a fortune — but you'll also have fun while making lots of money!

<u>**Your success can begin right now!**</u> All you have to do to start is look through your local paper for auction notices. You'll be surprised at how many bargains you can find right in your own home town!

Regardless of your interests, be they cars, jeeps, trucks, boats, planes, real estate, furniture, office supplies, antiques, stamps or collectibles, there are hundreds of auctions which will suit your needs!

What you have in your hands is an extremely powerful tool that is going to save you a fortune. Whether you simply want to save money on your next car, truck, or house, or if you want to quit your present job and make a very good living selling items you have bought at auction—this manual will show you exactly how and what to do.

In addition, your Volume 2 auction listing provides you with a state-by-state listing of various auctions being held across the United States. After you have finished reading through this directory and learning about the different kinds of auctions, the various agencies that sell surplus property, the types of property you can find at auction, and the auction terminology, you will want to refer to your Volume 2 auction listing. Remember that this is just a partial listing of the hundreds and hundreds of auctions that are held across the country every month!

We do strongly recommend that you read your Volume 1 directory thoroughly before proceeding to the Volume 2 auction listing. We realize you are anxious to start saving hundreds and even thousands of dollars by buying at auction! By carefully reading Volume 1 you will know where the best place will be to begin finding the types of auctions you want to attend for the items you wish to purchase!

Throughout this directory we have included photographs taken at auctions we have attended, as well as excerpts from various auction catalogs, advertisements, and newspaper ads. Remember—these are not photographs from new and used car lots—they are luxury cars, trucks, motorcycles, computers, etc. from actual auctions. This will give you an example of the types of quality merchandise that you will be finding at public auctions!

Did you realize that just about every branch of government holds some sort of sale to get rid of overstocked or unneeded merchandise? And what they sell varies from department to department, agency to agency. For instance, the DEA confiscates personal property from individuals who are trafficking in illegal drugs. This property includes everything from exotic automobiles and yachts to fabulous jewelry, artwork, furs, stamps, coins and even homes. When the U.S. Customs confiscates imported jewelry or leather goods, or the Department of Defense no longer needs a jeep, or the U.S. Marshals Service seizes a sports car from a drug dealer, all of these items can become available for purchase by the general public.

Add to this the enormous amount of property sold at State and local auctions, and you can easily see how, regardless of your interests or expertise, you're sure to find bargains through auctions and surplus sales! The possibilities are limitless — you set the guidelines and rules.

Cars, jeeps, exotics, boats, planes, houses, land, buildings, furniture, tools, condos, apartments — whatever you want — it's waiting for you. **Now it's time to get you more prepared than anyone else will be to really take advantage of the very real bargains offered every day as Uncle Sam "gives away" YOUR TAX DOLLARS!**

1971 STUTZ BLACKHAWK

1988 PONTIAC LEMANS

1987 FORD RANGER P/U

1958 FORD FAIRLANE

1984 MASERATI BI-TURBO

1984 NISSAN SENTRA

1989 DODGE COLT

1976 FORD F350 SUPER CAMPER SPECIAL

1987 CADILLAC ELDORADO

1988 BRITISH STERLING 825SL

1987 PONTIAC FIREBIRD

1984 LINCOLN CONTINENTAL MARK VII

1979 SCISSOR LIFT/DUMP TRUCK,
FORD FLATBEDS w/PIPE RACKING

FORD 8N TRACTORS (9N NOT PICTURED)

SOME OF THE CITY & COUNTY VEHICLES

Chapter 2:
Understanding Auctions

"My husband and I go to every auction we can attend. We love to collect antiques, and now thanks to our avid auction fever we have a house full! I'm seriously thinking of adding on to the house just to accomodate this hobby. What blows me away though, is that I even buy my garbage containers at auctions because I can get them cheaper than at any discount store! You just won't believe the bargains you find!"

T. Welker

For our purposes in this chapter we will deal with three basic types of auctions. Let's start out with the most common sort of auction — the PUBLIC AUCTION.

Public Auctions

This is the type of auction you will most often see advertised. At a public auction bids are made verbally and openly.

Registration is quite painless. You show your ID and then fill out a slip of paper which gives your name, address and phone number. You will then receive a card with your bidder's number on it. Some auctions give out 'ping pong' paddles with numbers on them. In some instances you will be required to pay a nominal registration fee, which is typically refunded in the event you don't buy anything.

BIDDING NUMBER

57

USE THIS CARD TO BID!

FOR YOUR PROTECTION
DO NOT LOSE THIS NUMBER

Make sure you keep your bidder's card (or paddle) with you. If you leave prior to the end of the auction, make sure you return the paddle. If you are using a bidder's card either tear it up into small pieces and dispose of it, or take it home with you and put it in the trash. You don't want someone else getting hold of your bidder's number and making offers. While this usually wouldn't cause you real problems—you don't want to be held responsible for a bid someone else made using your number!

While you are at the registration area, be sure to get a flyer, pamphlet or catalog which describes the items going up for auction.

The "condition of sale" will index the main characteristics of the auction. These typically include: form of payment and removal of merchandise. The conditions may also outline how bids will be accepted by the auctioneer.

Many newcomers buy items at auction without ever having inspected them. This is what separates the experienced buyer from the novice. Inspections are generally encouraged at most auctions. The inspection period may vary from an hour before the auction to a week prior to the actual sale. Be sure to take this time and use it wisely, since obviously you should never buy something strictly on impulse. **Period.** No exceptions!

Items are sold at auction "as is," with no guarantees. If you purchase a boat, plane, automobile, house or other "big ticket" item, you'd best plan in advance how you are going to move this newly purchased property—and what expense will be involved.

An interesting, although extreme, example of the cost of moving a bargain purchase occurred not too long ago in the city of Des Moines, Iowa. A complete block of Victorian homes could be purchased for $1.00 each. There was only one catch — you had to be able to move them to another location!

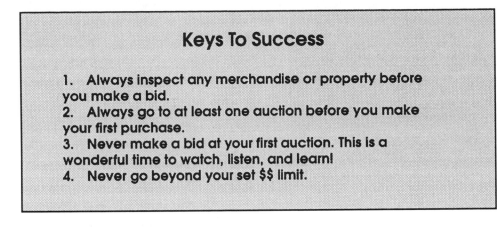

Keys To Success

1. Always inspect any merchandise or property before you make a bid.
2. Always go to at least one auction before you make your first purchase.
3. Never make a bid at your first auction. This is a wonderful time to watch, listen, and learn!
4. Never go beyond your set $$ limit.

Sealed Bid Auctions

These auctions are generally done almost entirely through the mail. Government agencies will sometimes allow you to fax a "sealed bid," but all sealed bids are made in writing. The major drawback with this type of auction is that no one bidding has any idea of what is going on. Bidders don't know if they've had the successful bid until all of the sealed bids have been tallied. Sometimes this can take days.

While this is not the most popular form of "auction," there are some governmental agencies & auctioneers who use this method. Some of the governmental agencies print catalogs of what will be sold by sealed bid. These are called Invitations for Bids (IFB).

There are not usually set schedules when governmental agencies will hold a sealed bid auction. Some agencies schedule them regularly, holding an auction every few weeks or once a month, while others hold auctions only when the need arises.

For example, the Department of Housing and Urban Development (HUD) advertises their sealed bid auctions in the classified section of many local weekend newspapers. HUD doesn't provide a catalog, but they do list the real estate they have for sale in these ads.

When you receive catalogs for upcoming sealed bid sales, they will give you a brief description of the merchandise being sold. This often includes the condition and quantities of the items being auctioned.

Be sure to pay attention to this information so you know exactly how many of an item you are bidding on. If they are auctioning off a lot of 300 television sets or typewriters and you only need one, you won't want to waste time bidding. However, it might be to your advantage to contact the successful bidder on the lot of typewriters or television sets and let him know you are interested in purchasing one. Since he just purchased them for a bargain price he may be willing to sell you one for just slightly higher than his unit cost—especially since he knows that you are aware he purchased them at auction and got a great deal on them.

The sealed bid catalog will include a bid form. There is a sheet which will give you the necessary instructions for making your bid. There may be a short paragraph or several pages—**READ THEM CAREFULLY.**

You will find the address where your bid must be sent on either the front page of the catalog or on the actual bidding sheet. In addition, you will also see a deadline date and time for when your bid must be received. Bids arriving after the deadline aren't accepted.

Some agencies require that you send a deposit with your bid. The deposit may be as high as 20% of your bid. Money orders, cashier's checks and certified checks are standard methods of payment. A few agencies allow the deposit to be made via credit card.

You might be saying, "Wait a minute, who would bid on something sight unseen?" Don't worry. There is a preview period at sealed bid auctions, too. You will have the opportunity to personally inspect the merchandise prior to making your bid. Generally speaking, you will have a longer time period in which to inspect merchandise than you would at a public auction. **IT IS VERY IMPORTANT THAT YOU INSPECT ANYTHING YOU MAY BE THINKING OF BIDDING ON.** If you cannot personally inspect it, at least send a friend who can. Suppose the merchandise is in another state? Many catalogs will provide a listing for a contact person. This individual is the custodian for that property. You can call this person and make inquiries with regard to the items you wish to purchase.

Spot Bid Auctions

In some respects the spot bid auction is kind of a cross between the verbal public auction and the sealed bid sale. At this type of auction an item is offered as usual, but then the bidders write down their bid on a bid form. All written bids are collected, and the winning bid is announced publicly.

The spot bid auctions can have both advantages and disadvantages. At this type of auction you will need to rely on your own expertise and expectations of what you are willing to pay a bit more than you might at another type of auction. For example, picture yourself at an auction. You are planning to bid on the cream colored Ford Ranger pick-up. You hope to be able to purchase the pick-up for $600, but are willing to go as high as $800 for the truck. This is a verbal auction, and when it's time to bid on this truck  you offer the opening bid of $400. The auctioneer starts working the crowd, but there doesn't seem to be anyone else interested in this pick-up. The other people in the crowd had really gone wild over a Firebird that was offered earlier, and there is another Firebird coming up after the pick-up, so it appears the others are holding off in order to bid on the Firebird. Going, going, GONE! You have the winning bid on the pick-up for $400!

At the spot bid auction you have no idea how much others are bidding for an item, so you cannot base your bid according to theirs. You get one chance to bid on an item. In the example of the Ford Ranger pick-up, you might bid your top price of $800 in order to stand more of a chance of getting the pick-up, and have no way of knowing if the next-higher bid had been $400 or $795.

At most spot bid auctions the bids for each lot will be collected individually and the winning bid announced before the start of the bidding for the next lot. Occasionally you may attend a spot bid auction where the bids are collected and all winning bids are announced at the end. If you attend a spot bid auction and aren't clear when the winning bids will be announced, make sure you ask before bidding starts.

Chapter 3:
Your "Jump-Start"
Auction Program

> "I've been in the auction business for over 30 years. I've sold just about everything under the sun at one time or another. The auction is certainly free enterprise at work on a very basic scale! I've seen people buy items at unbelievably low prices. Sure, I'm in the business to make money for the seller and myself—but there's plenty of room for everyone to come out in good shape. And the best part is, it's lots of fun!"
>
> J. Carpenter

When you purchased this directory, you were ready to start buying incredible bargains at auctions, right? This chapter is designed to get you off and running **right now.** There is no reason to wait. All you need to do is follow the directions in this section and you will already be on the road to success!

Here is an easy guideline which will give you step-by-step key information so that you will be able to attend your first auction within the next two weeks:

Step One:

First you need to contact three or four agencies who hold auctions on a regular basis. There are a lot of government and private agencies holding auctions all the time. For your purposes, let's start with one of the agencies closest to home. Take a look at the state-by-state listings throughout this directory. Find your state and contact the agency listed. Ask to get on their mailing list. Most likely, they will have an auction coming up in the near future which you can attend. While you are talking to them, you can ask them to send you a <u>successful bidders list,</u> which will allow you to see the kinds of bargains people attending these auctions have been getting. We show you a sample of a successful bidder's list on pages 193-194.

When you're done talking to the people in your state, it's time to get hold of some governmental agencies. You will want to contact the General Services Administration (GSA), the Defense Reutilization Marketing Office (DRMO), and the U.S. Customs Service (Auctioneer: EG&G Dynatrend), since each of these agencies hold auctions **ALL THE TIME!**

You may want to take a moment now to fill in the information in the spaces below. In this way you will have the information at-hand for quick reference in the future.

U.S. Customs Service—EG&G Dynatrend
Cars, boats, airplanes, furs, jewelry, antiques, collectibles, and lots more. (See pages 97-101)
Local Office In My Area:_____
Address:_____
City/State:_____ Zip:_____
Phone:_____Contact: _____

Defense Reutilization Marketing Office
Electronics, hardware, paint, computers, machines, office equipment, aircraft, scrap metal, and much, much more. (See pages 121-133.)
Local Office In My Area:_____
Address:_____
City/State:_____ Zip:_____
Phone:_____Contact: _____

General Services Administration
Cars, car parts, electronics, furniture, office furniture and equipment, kitchen equipment, and a lot more. (See pages 103-115)

Local Office In My Area:_____

Address:_____

City/State:_____Zip: _____

Phone:_____Contact: _____

Step Two:

You will want to contact these three agencies above right away! Since auctions are held all the time, you'll want to be sure you don't miss out on upcoming opportunities! The easiest and fastest way to contact them is by phone. Some of these agencies even have FAX capabilities, so you can get your request to them in writing immediately. It should only take you a few minutes to contact them, and as soon as you do you will begin receiving flyers advising you of upcoming auctions. If you find it necessary to send a letter, the following will give you a good outline to use:

Dear (Name of Agency);

I would like information on any upcoming auctions or sales your agency is holding in my area (be sure to name ALL areas which interest you at this point).

If you have a mailing list, please add my name to it so that I can continue to receive information on your sales. I am enclosing a self-addressed, stamped envelope for your convenience.

Thanks so much for your help! I look forward to hearing from you soon.

Sincerely,

Your Signature
Your Name
Your Address

Step Three:

It's smart to send a <u>self-addressed, stamped envelope!</u> Any time you are writing a letter asking for auction lists, it's a good idea to include an envelope which is addressed back to you and stamped. In this way, if you contact an agency which is overworked — or which has a backlog of requests — your request will be easy (and quick) for them to respond to. Note: Make sure you use a #10 legal size envelope.

Step Four:

Start checking your <u>local newspaper.</u> Regardless of where you live, your local and regional papers will be a wealth of information about upcoming auctions. You can call your local newspaper and talk to the people working in the classified and display advertising departments to find out if there is one particular day of the week devoted to auction notices. Many newspapers have a long list of auction notices in their Sunday editions.

For those of you living in Northern California, there is a big auction house located in Modesto that turns out very good auctions. In addition to the other agencies listed throughout this directory, you may wish to contact them and ask to be placed on their mailing list to receive flyers for upcoming auctions. Contact them at:

Roger Ernst & Associates
P.O. Box 3251
Modesto, CA 95353
(209) 527-7399

Your Best Information May Come From a Phone Call

One of the quickest ways to get information is to pick up the phone and call the agency or auctioneer for direct communication. If you are lucky enough to have a FAX machine available, you may wish to submit a letter of inquiry by that method. The example letter presented on the previous page would be fine to send as a FAX to an agency you are trying to get information from.

If you are going to use the phone, there are some general rules of thumb you'll want to abide by as much as possible. <u>**Always be polite,**</u> and try to remember that the person on the other end of the line probably has lots of other jobs and duties to perform — so your call is not necessarily a real priority to them.

Let's pretend you're making a phone call right now. Here's how it should go:

- Hi, this is **YOUR NAME** and I'm trying to get some information about upcoming auctions.

- Should I talk to you, or is there someone else who handles this? **WHEN YOU HAVE THE RIGHT PERSON,** then:

- Thanks for your time. I understand you specialize in **(TYPE OF AUCTIONS)** and I'm interested in attending auctions you may be having in my area. Do you have a mailing list? (If they do, this is the time to ask for your name & address to be included.)

- Do you do any work for the State or Federal government? **If the answer is 'yes', then:** What types of goods do you sell for them?

- Do you know of other auction houses I can call that will be selling the types of items I am looking for?

- Do you keep a successful bidders list? If so, is it possible for me to get a copy of a couple from previous auctions?

- Thanks for your help! I'll look forward to receiving the information I've requested soon.

Smart Tip

Any time you send a self-addressed, stamped, envelope (SASE) when requesting information, make sure you use a #10 legal size envelope. It will make it easier for whoever fills your request. Also make sure to always print your name and address neatly and in ink.

Santa Barbara Police Auction

When:
Saturday, December 17

Viewing Time:
9am-10am
Sale to Start at 10am.

Where:
Police Department

PRIDE
OBJECTIVITY
LEADERSHIP
INTEGRITY
COMMITMENT
EXCELLENCE
SANTA BARBARA

Santa Barbara's Police Department's Explorer Post will have refreshments as a fundraiser.

Bicycles, Jewelry, Radios & many other items.

Local Checks accepted with I.D. All sales final. Items sold as is.
*Jewelry viewing is limited to 5 minutes per group.

In the event of rain, the auction will be January 7th

Chapter 4:
City Police Auctions

"You gotta know what you're buying—watch what you buy and know when to stop bidding. Dealers sometimes bump the bids to discourage private parties. You gotta be willing to go to the next auction if you aren't able to get what you want for the price you want. There is always another chance."

M. Laurie

The merchandise available at auction through your local police department will depend upon the size of the community in which you live. Obviously, the larger metropolitan areas are going to have more available, and hold auctions more frequently, than the small town.

What's available is there because of insurance claims on unrecovered property, failure of crime victims to file police reports, and stiff fines for parking violations. Large cities need to empty their storage facilities so they have room for newly confiscated items. In these areas monthly auctions are not uncommon.

Many of the larger police departments use the services of professional auctioneers to sell off their abandoned property. In smaller towns and cities the police officers may handle the auction themselves.

What will you find at a police auction? Whatever items are routinely involved in crimes. They might include confiscated cars, jewelry, TVs, VCRs, radios, camera equipment, car stereos and speakers, computers—just about anything a burglar might have in his or her possession when arrested. For some reason, bicycles also find their way to police auctions in droves.

In coastal communities you may also find boats being auctioned. Like cars, these have either been abandoned or have incurred a violation against them which the owner was unable to pay.

To make it easier for you to find out about upcoming auctions, several police departments have even set up auction hotline messages for interested buyers. If a professional auctioneer is handling the sale, you should be able to get a flier.

Bargains can abound at these auctions. You can often pick up cars for at most a few hundred dollars. Television sets sell for as low as $30, and bikes often sell for as little as $2 or $3!

At most, if not all, police auctions, the vehicles are sold "as is/where is", and they mean it! At many auctions you can't start them up, you can't open the hood, you can't even open the door and look inside. In many instances you'll have to have a locksmith make a key so you can take the car. What does this mean to you? This sometimes keeps others from bidding, so you often can get incredible bargains. Be as thorough as you can and bid very low. A good rule of thumb is to never pay more than you could get back by selling the parts. You may very well get a real steal!

Insider's Tip

One of the auctioneers we interviewed for this manual gave us a tip to pass along to you:

Call the DMV in the area where you plan to attend an auction and see if they ever have any problems with transferring title for cars purchased at Police Auctions to the new buyer (YOU). Usually this is no problem.... but very rarely people have problems securing title to cars bought at Police Auctions because the cars have been confiscated and the title is not available. It's best to double check before you put any money down!

Your best bet for locating City Police Auctions will be your local phone directory. Take a look in the white pages under the City Government listing and call their non-emergency number. Once you have someone on the phone, explain to them that you are interested in finding out more about any auctions they may hold. Don't forget to ask to be included on their mailing list, if one is maintained. Find out how they advertise their sales and how frequently they are held.

If you don't mind driving, then you'll want to check with the City Police Departments in neighboring areas. You'll likely be surprised by just how many areas hold auctions. If you are particularly interested in cars, be sure to ask the various agencies you talk to if they know of an area close by which might have more cars available at auction.

It never hurts to ask questions—and many times this will be the best way you have of finding out about future sales, or particular types of sales in which you would be interested.

In our Chapter 16: Be A Pro—Auction Insider Secrets, we discuss purchase strategies and offer advice on things to look for when purchasing a car. This includes mechanical information as well as pricing information. You will want to make sure you read that chapter before attending a City Police Auction or other type of auction with the intent of purchasing a car, truck, pick-up, van, 4 × 4 or other type of transportation.

Smart Tip

Any time you are buying a car without the ability to start it up and/or make sure it is truly road worthy, your best bet is not to bid more than you could get if you sold it for parts.

1989 FORD RANGER PICKUP

1989 PLYMOUTH SUNDANCE

1987 NISSAN PICKUP

1985 FORD 30 PASS. VAN

1990 ENCOUNTER MOTOR HOME

1986 FORD 1 TON UTILITY TRUCK

1989 FORD ½ TON VAN

1987 CHRYSLER LE BARON

1987 MITSUBISHI PICKUP

1986 GMC CABALLERO

1988 CHEVROLET ASTRO VAN

1987 CHEVROLET S-10 PICKUP

1987 JEEP WRANGLER

1987 MAZDA RX7

1987 NISSAN MAXIMA

1979 CADILLAC SEVILLE

1980 PETERBILT
TRUCK TRACTOR

1975 PETERBILT CB200
TRUCK TRACTOR

1985 BUICK LE SABRE

1985 CHEVROLET S-10 BLAZER

1986 CHEVROLET 1 TON
STAKEBED TRUCK

1984 BMW 318i

1990 PLYMOUTH LASER

1986 CHEVROLET EL CAMINO

1991 FORD 11 PASS. VAN

1986 PLYMOUTH VOYAGER VAN

ADDITIONAL ITEMS ARE BEING ADDED DAILY!

1993 LEXUS LS400

1979 ROLLS ROYCE SILVER
SHADOW

1990 ACURA INTEGRA

1991 FORD MUSTANG 5.0

1991 HARLEY DAVIDSON
CUSTOM SOFTAIL

1989 HONDA 500R
MOTORCYCLE

1989 KAWASAKI NINJA
MOTORCYCLE

1991 CHEVROLET 1 TON PICKUP

1987 CHEVROLET CORVETTE

1986 FORD THUNDERBIRD ELAN

1979 CHEVROLET CORVETTE

ADDITIONAL ITEMS ARE BEING ADDED DAILY!

Chapter 5:
United States Trustees
Bankruptcy Auctions

"I go to a lot of auctions. I go to Vandenberg, I go up North, I go to Cal Trans, bankruptcies…I go to a lot of 'em. I've been going to auctions for 20 years. I buy for personal and I sell at the swap meet. I buy vehicles, too. I buy them anywhere from $50 up. I get a lot of deals."

L. Day

Although the United States Trustee program is designed to appoint and oversee bankruptcy trustees in regional districts across the country, most of the real business is conducted by outside auctioneers. The Bankruptcy Trustees are usually so overloaded with work that they welcome the help of an auctioneer. The Trustee may handle the paperwork, and leave everything else in the hands of this auctioneer.

The number of auctions has risen dramatically, due to the growing number of bankruptcies each year. Well over a million individuals and companies accept protection under the U.S. Bankruptcy laws each year.

There are several methods for getting information on bankruptcy auctions:

- You can check the classified section of your local newspaper for information on upcoming sales. You can look in your phone book's yellow pages under Auctioneer and make some phone calls to find out who handles bankruptcy auctions in your area.

• You can also contact the U.S. Trustee in your area (see list on following pages) and ask them for a list of bankruptcy trustees near where you live. Sometimes this requires going physically to their office to copy the information—but they will usually mail it to you.

Once you have the list you can telephone the bankruptcy trustees in your area and ask them for the name and number of the auctioneer they use. Once you have this information, all you do is call the auctioneer and request to be added to his mailing list.

When the restaurant I owned went bankrupt in 1992, I had well over $200,000 worth of equipment and inventory. Guess what the total brought in at the bankruptcy auction was? Are you sitting down? The auction brought in $19,132. That's right, $200,000 worth of merchandise was sold for less than $20,000. That's less than 10 cents on the dollar. And this was good equipment less than one year old. It's not hard to see that someone made out like a bandit. Now, just think about how many times this scenario is played out every day across the United States. This truly presents incredible opportunities for bargain hunters!

Bankruptcy auctions are probably the best auctions you can attend. There are tremendous opportunities for individuals who buy at bankruptcy auctions.

Many careers are started by attending these auctions. Reselling is much easier if you have purchased the items at a great price to start with.

Regardless of what you're interested in—boats, planes, vehicles, computers, office equipment, furs, jewelry, furniture, artwork, coins, etc.—somewhere, someplace, you'll find an auctioneer selling just what you're looking for!

> ## Smart Tip
>
> Some newcomers worry that bankruptcy auctions are "subject to court confirmation." Never fear. The majority of federal bankruptcy judges are so overwhelmed with work that they very rarely require proof of fair market value.

Bankruptcy Trustees

Region 1: Massaschusetts, Maine, New Hampshire, Rhode Island

U.S. Trustee: 10 Causeway St., Room 1184; Boston, MA 02222-1043
(617) 565-6360, FAX (617) 565-6368

Assistant U.S. Trustee: 537 Congress St., Suite 303; Portland, ME 04101
(207) 780-3564, FAX (207) 780-3568

Assistant U.S. Trustee: 66 Hanover St., Suite 302; Manchester, NH 03101
(603) 666-7908, FAX (603) 666-7913

Region 2: Connecticut, New York, Vermont

U.S. Trustee: 80 Broad St., Third Floor; New York, NY 10004
(212) 668-2200, FAX (212) 668-2256

Assistant U.S. Trustee: 825 E. Gate Blvd., Suite 304; Garden City, NY 11530
(718) 553-7071, FAX (718) 553-7052

Assistant U.S. Trustee: 42 Delaware Ave., Suite 100; Buffalo, NY 14202
(716) 551-5541, FAX (716) 551-5560

Assistant U.S. Trustee: 105 Court St., Suite 403; New Haven, CT 06511
(203) 773-2210, FAX (203) 773-2217

Region 3: Delaware, New Jersey, Pennsylvania

U.S. Trustee: 601 Walnut St., Room 950W; Philadelphia, PA 19106
(215) 597-4411, FAX (215) 597-5795

Assistant U.S. Trustee: 1000 Liberty Ave., Room 319, Pittsburgh, PA 15222
(412) 644-4756, FAX (412) 644-4785

Assistant U.S. Trustee: 225 Market St., Suite 503; Harrisburg, PA 17101
(717) 782-4907, FAX (717) 782-4927

Assistant U.S. Trustee: One Newark Center, Suite 2100; Newark, NJ 07102
(201) 645-3014, FAX (201) 645-5993

Region 4: District of Columbia, Maryland, North Carolina, South Carolina, Virgin Islands, West Virginia

U.S. Trustee: 1201 Main St., Room 2440; Columbia, SC 29201
(803) 806-3001

Assistant U.S. Trustee: 115 S. Union St., Room 210; Alexandria, VA 22314
(703) 557-7176, FAX (703) 557-7279

Assistant U.S. Trustee: 200 Granby St., Room 625; Norfolk, VA 23510
(804) 441-6012, FAX (804) 441-3266

Assistant U.S. Trustee: 280 Franklin Rd. SW, Room 806; Roanoke, VA24011-2212
(703) 857-2806, FAX (703) 857-2844

Assistant U.S. Trustee: 500 Virginia St. East, Room 590; Charleston, WV 25301
(304) 347-5310, FAX (304) 347-5316

Assistant U.S. Trustee: 6305 Ivy Lane, Suite 600, Greenbelt, MD 20770
(301) 344-6216, FAX (301) 344-8431

Assistant U.S. Trustee: 300 W. Pratt St., Suite 350, Baltimore, MD 21201
(410) 962-3910, FAX (410) 962-4278

Region 5: Louisiana, Mississippi

U.S. Trustee: 400 Poydras St., Suite 2110; New Orleans, LA 70130
(504) 589-4018, FAX (504) 589-4096

Assistant U.S. Trustee: 300 Fannin St., Suite 3196; Shreveport, LA 71101
(318) 676-3456, FAX (318) 676-3212

Assistant U.S. Trustee: 100 W. Capital St., Suite 1232; Jackson, MS 39269
(601) 965-5241, FAX (601) 965-8226

Panel Trustee: P.O. Box 5918, Suite 135; Metairie, LA 70009
(504) 586-9403

Panel Trustee: 7906 Wrenwood Blvd., Suite A; Baton Rouge, LA 70809
(504) 928-9520

Panel Trustee: P.O. Box 729; New Albany, MS 38652
(601) 534-9581

Panel Trustee: 4812 Jefferson Avenue; Gulfport, MS 39501
(601) 864-1100

Region 6: Texas, Northern and Eastern Districts

U.S. Trustee: 1100 Commerce St., Room 9C60; Dallas, TX 75242
(214) 767-8967, FAX (214) 767-8971

Assistant U.S. Trustee: 110 N. College Ave., Room 300; Tyler, TX 75702
(903) 597-8312, FAX (903) 597-9700

Region 7: Texas, Southern and Western Districts

U.S. Trustee: 440 Louisiana St., Suite 2500; Houston, TX 77002
(713) 238-9650, FAX (713) 238-9670

Assistant U.S. Trustee: 615 E. Houston St., Suite 533, San Antonio, TX 78205 (210)
229-4640, FAX (210) 229-4649

Assistant U.S. Trustee: 300 E. 8th St., Room 906; Austin, TX 78701
(512) 482-5328, FAX (512) 482-5331

Region 8: Kentucky, Tennessee

U.S. Trustee: 200 Jefferson Ave., Suite 400; Memphis, TN 38103
(901) 544-3251, FAX (901) 544-4138

Assistant U.S. Trustee: 31 E. 11th St., 4th Floor; Chattanooga, TN 37402
(615) 752-5153, FAX (615) 752-5161

Assistant U.S. Trustee: 701 Broadway, Room 318; Nashville, TN 37203
(615) 736-2254, FAX (615) 736-2260

Assistant U.S. Trustee: 601 W. Broadway, Suite 512; Louisville, KY 40202
(502) 582-6000, FAX (502) 582-6147

Assistant U.S. Trustee: 100 E. Vine St., Suite 803; Lexington, KY 40507
(606) 233-2822, FAX (606) 233-2834

Region 9: Michigan, Ohio

U.S. Trustee: 200 Public Square, 20th Floor, Suite 3300; Cleveland, OH 44114
(216) 522-7800, FAX (216) 522-4988

Assistant U.S. Trustee: 50 W. Broad St., Suite 325; Columbus, OH 43215
(614) 469-7411, FAX (614) 469-7448

Assistant U.S. Trustee: 330 Ionia NW, Suite 202; Grand Rapids, MI 49503
(616) 456-2002, FAX (616) 456-2550

Assistant U.S. Trustee: 477 Michigan Ave., Room 1760; Detroit, MI 48226
(313) 226-7999, FAX (313) 226-7952

Region 10: Indiana, Illinois (Central & Southern Districts)

U.S. Trustee: 101 W. Ohio St., Room 1000; Indianapolis, IN 46204
(317) 226-6101, FAX (317) 226-6356

Assistant U.S. Trustee: 100 E. Wayne St., Room 555; South Bend, IN 46601
(219) 236-8105, FAX (219) 236-8163

Assistant U.S. Trustee: 100 NE Monroe St., Room 311; Peoria, IL 61602
(309) 671-7854, FAX (309) 671-7857

Region 11: Wisconsin, Illinois (Northern District)

U.S. Trustee: 227 W. Monroe St., Suite 3350; Chicago, IL 60606
(312) 886-5785, FAX (312) 886-5794

Assistant U.S. Trustee: 14 W. Mifflin St., Room 310; Madison, WI 53703
(608) 264-5522, FAX (608) 264-5182

Assistant U.S. Trustee: 517 E. Wisconsin Ave., Room 430; Milwaukee, WI
53202 (414) 297-4499, FAX (414) 297-4478

Region 12: Iowa, Minnesota, North Dakota, South Dakota

U.S. Trustee: 225 Second St. SE, Suite 400, Cedar Rapids, IA 52401
(319) 364-2211, FAX (319) 364-7370

Assistant U.S. Trustee: 210 Walnut St., Suite 517; Des Moines, IA 50309-2108
(515) 284-4982, FAX (515) 284-4986

Assistant U.S. Trustee: 331 Second Ave. S, Suite 540, Minneapolis, MN 55401
(612) 373-1200, FAX (612) 373-1216

Assistant U.S. Trustee: 230 S. Philips Ave., Suite 502, Sioux Falls, SD 57102
(605) 330-4450, FAX (605) 330-4456

Panel Trustee: 12 S. Main St. #202; Minot, ND 58701
(701) 838-9422

Panel Trustee: 750 Pierce St., P.O. Box 717, Sioux City, IA 51102
(712) 277-1015

Panel Trustee: 101 E. Fifth St., Suite 1614; St. Paul, MN 55101-1808
(612) 224-3361

Region 13: Arkansas, Nebraska, Missouri

U.S. Trustee: 911 Walnut St., Room 806; Kansas City, MO 64106
(816) 426-7959, FAX (816) 426-7967

Assistant U.S. Trustee: 815 Olive St., Room 412; St. Louis, MO 63101
(314) 539-2976, FAX (314) 539-2990

Assistant U.S. Trustee: 210 S. 16th St., Suite 560; Omaha, NE 68102
(402) 221-4300, FAX (402) 221-4383

Assistant U.S. Trustee: 500 S. Broadway, Suite 201; Little Rock, AR 72201
(501) 324-7357, FAX (501) 324-7388

Panel Trustee: P.O. Box 7628; Columbia, MO 65205
(314) 442-4011, FAX (314) 875-2521

Panel Trustee: P.O. Box 50280; Springfield, MO 65805
(417) 864-7772, FAX (417) 864-7894

Region 14: Arizona

U.S. Trustee: 320 N. Central Ave., Room 100; Phoenix, AZ 85004
(602) 379-3092, FAX (602) 379-3242

Panel Trustee: P.O. Box 5478; Mesa, Az 85211-5478
(602) 844-1624

Panel Trustee: P.O. Box 32967, Phoenix, AZ 85064-2967
(602) 956-2218, FAX (602) 955-5902

Panel Trustee: 1202 Willow Creek Rd., Suite B; Prescott, AZ 86301
(602) 778-3132, FAX (602) 778-5453

Panel Trustee: 221 S. Second Ave., Yuma, AZ 85364
(602) 783-7809, FAX (602) 783-7800

Panel Trustee: 4730 N. Oracle, Suite 218; Tucson, AZ 85705
(602) 293-1226, FAX (602) 293-1302

Region 15: California (Southern District), Hawaii, Guam

U.S. Trustee: 101 S. Broadway, Suite 440; San Diego, CA 92101
(619) 557-5013, FAX (619) 557-5339

Assistant U.S. Trustee: 300 Ala Moana Blvd., Room 6321B; Honolulu, HI 96850
(808) 541-3360, FAX (808) 541-3367

Assistant U.S. Trustee: 238 Archbishop Flores, Room 805; Agana, Guam 96910
(671) 472-7736, FAX (671) 472-7344

Region 16: California (Central District)

U.S. Trustee: 221 N. Figueroa, Suite 800; Los Angeles, CA 90012
(213) 894-6811, FAX (213) 894-2603

Assistant U.S. Trustee: 600 W. Santa Ana Blvd., Room 501; Santa Ana, CA
92701 (714) 836-2691, FAX (714) 836-2881

Assistant U.S. Trustee: 699 N. Arrowhead Ave., Rm. 106; San Bernardino, CA
92401 (909) 383-5850, FAX (909) 383-5861

Panel Trustee: 11150 Olympic Blvd. #940; Los Angeles, CA 90064

Region 17: California (Eastern & Northern Districts), Nevada

U.S. Trustee: 250 Montgomery St., Suite 910; San Francisco, CA 94104
(415) 705-3300, FAX (415) 705-3367 (Send a Self-address, Stamped envelope)

Assistant U.S. Trustee: 1301 Clay St., Suite 690N; Oakland, CA 94612
(510) 637-3200, FAX (510) 637-3220

Assistant U.S. Trustee: 280 S. First St., Room 268; San Jose, CA 95113
(408) 535-5525 , FAX (408) 291-7459

Assistant U.S. Trustee: 915 "L" St., Suite 1150; Sacramento, CA 95814
(916) 498-5990, FAX (916) 498-5995

Assistant U.S. Trustee: 1130 "O" St., Suite 1110; Fresno, CA 93721
(209) 487-5400, FAX (209) 487-5401

Assistant U.S. Trustee: 600 Las Vegas Blvd. S, Suite 430; Las Vegas, NV 89101
(702) 388-6600, FAX (702) 388-6658

Assistant U.S. Trustee: 350 S. Center St., Suite 280; Reno, NV 89501
(702) 784-5335, FAX (702) 784-5531

Region 18: Alaska, Idaho, Montana, Oregon, Washington

U.S. Trustee: 1200 6th Ave., Room 600; Seattle, WA 98101
(206) 553-2000, FAX (206) 553-2566

Assistant U.S. Trustee: N. 221 Wall St., Suite 538, Spokane, WA 99201
(509) 353-2999, FAX (509) 353-3124

Assistant U.S. Trustee: 851 SW 6th Ave., Suite 1300; Portland, OR 97204
(503) 326-4000, FAX (503) 326-7658

Assistant U.S. Trustee: 301 Central Ave., Suite 204; Great Falls, MT 59401
(406) 761-8777, FAX (406) 761-8895

Assistant U.S. Trustee: 304 N. Eighth St., Room 347; Boise, ID 83702
(208) 334-1300, FAX (208) 334-9756

Assistant U.S. Trustee: 605 W. 4th. Ave., Suite 258, Anchorage, AK 99501
(907) 271-2600, FAX (907) 271-2610

Region 19: Colorado, Utah, Wyoming

U.S. Trustee: 721 19th St., Suite 408; Denver, CO 80202
(303) 844-5188, FAX (303) 844-5230

Assistant U.S. Trustee: 9 Exchange Pl., Suite 100; Salt Lake City, UT 84111
(801) 524-5734, FAX (801) 524-5628

Assistant U.S. Trustee: 200 W. 17th St., Room 310; Cheyenne, WY 82001
(307) 772-2790, FAX (307) 772-2795

Region 20: Kansas, New Mexico, Oklahoma

U.S. Trustee: 401 N. Market St., Room 180; Wichita, KS 67202
(316) 269-6637, FAX (316) 269-6182

Assistant U.S. Trustee: 224 S. Boulder, Room 225; Tulsa, OK 74103
(918) 581-6670, FAX (918) 581-6674

Assistant U.S. Trustee: 215 Dean A. McGee Ave., Room 408; Oklahoma City,
OK 73102 (405) 231-5950, FAX (405) 231-5958

Assistant U.S. Trustee: 421
Gold St. SW, Suite 112;
Albuquerque, NM 87102
(505) 248-6544

Panel Trustee: 5101 N.
Classen, Suite 204,
Oklahoma City, OK 73118
(405) 842-8083, 842-3083

Panel Trustee: 301 W.
Central; Wichita, KS 67202

Panel Trustee: 11900
College Blvd., Suite 341, Overland Park, KS 66210

Region 21: Alabama, Florida, Georgia, Puerto Rico, Virgin Islands

U.S. Trustee: 75 Spring St. SW, Room 3362; Atlanta, GA 30303
(404) 331-4437, FAX (404) 331-4464

Assistant U.S. Trustee: 222 W. Oglethorpe Ave., Suite 302; Savannah, GA 31401
(912) 652-4112, FAX (912) 652-4123

Assistant U.S. Trustee: 433 Cherry St., Suite 510; Macon, GA 31201
(912) 752-3544, FAX (912) 752-3549

Assistant U.S. Trustee: 227 N. Bronough St., Room 1038, Tallahassee, FL 32301
(904) 942-8899, FAX (904) 942-8345

Assistant U.S. Trustee: 135 W. Central Blvd., Suite 620; Orlando, FL 32801
(407) 648-6301, FAX (407) 648-6323

Assistant U.S. Trustee: Chardon St., Room 638; Hato Rey, PR 00918 (809) 766-5851, FAX (809) 766-6250

14KT WHITE GOLD RING w/2.88 CARAT DIAMOND

SOME OF THE MANY REMOTE CONTROL CARS AND TRUCKS

SPORTS COLLECTIBLES

MANY HOSES, STRAPS, ETC.

RAIN OR SHINE

HOUSEHOLD ITEMS & MISCELLANEOUS

JUST SOME OF THE ITEMS IN THE DECEMBER SALE:

ROCKING HORSES
DINING ROOM SETS
REMOTE CONTROL CARS & TRUCKS
SURPLUS COMPUTER EQUIPMENT
LARGE SELECTION OF JEWELRY
TV's • LIVING ROOM FURNITURE
NEW DISH SETS • TRAIN SETS
PALLET RACKING SHELVING
SMALL KITCHEN APPLIANCES
LAMPS • SPORTS COLLECTIBLES
COINS • CAR STEREOS
TABLES/CURIO STANDS
MIRRORS • SPORTS CARDS
BIG SCREEN TV's
COMPLETE COMPUTER SYSTEMS
COPY MACHINES
RESTAURANT EQUIPMENT
SHRINK WRAP MACHINE
HALL'S 2-DR. VERTICAL SAFE (4'x7')
POOL CUES • VCR's
OFFICE EQUIPMENT
CUTLERY SETS • LUGGAGE
HOME STEREO SYSTEMS
METAL CARTS • STORAGE CABINETS
IBM SELECTRIC II TYPEWRITERS
COFFEE AND END TABLES • TOYS
COLLECTIBLE DAGGERS & SWORDS
LEATHER JACKETS
WALL HEATERS
OLYMPIC WEIGHT SETS
METAL GYM LOCKERS
PORTABLE SALAD BARS

ONE OF THREE ROLEX WATCHES

ROCKING HORSES

ONE OF MANY TRAIN SETS

NEW DISH & COOKWARE SETS

SOME OF THE MANY HAND & POWER TOOLS

Chapter 6:
Personal Surplus Sales

"Every year my husband and I have at least 5 or 6 garage sales. We spend our free weekends going to swap meets, auctions, garage and yard sales—even the Goodwill and Salvation Army stores. It's amazing how many things you can pick up for a song. Then all you do is mark the price up a bit and resell the items. We always make between $300 and $500 any time we hold a sale. Our hobby allows us to buy some of life's little luxuries—and we have loads of fun, too!"

K. DuBois

L et's not overlook the most popular and common auctions of all time. Rather than call them "Garage Sales" or "Yard Sales," we are going to call them "PERSONAL SURPLUS SALES." And EVERYONE has something that can be called "PERSONAL SURPLUS"!

Regardless of the size community you live in, there are sure to be lots of garage and yard sales each and every weekend. In the colder climates these tend to take place when spring arrives—and they continue well into the fall. In warmer areas, sales go on year 'round. Do you think all of these sales are simply items that individual families have found in their basements, attics and garages? WRONG. Many people make a good living by scouting other sales for bargains and then turning around and reselling their items for a handsome profit. Imagine making good money doing something you love!!

The first step you need to take is to do a personal inventory of items in your possession right this minute which could easily be sold through a "PERSONAL SURPLUS SALE". How about that old bike in the garage? Or maybe the set of tires you keep thinking will come in handy? Perhaps you have some discarded furniture or bedding, an old lamp, some shoes, throw

rugs that just don't match your carpet? Hardly a home exists which doesn't have a ton of already read paperback books taking up way too much space! Now that you've got cassettes and CDs—how much space are your old records taking up? When was the last time you listened to them? You get the idea—your junk may very well be someone else's treasure.

If you've never had a "PERSONAL SURPLUS SALE", it's very easy to get started. First, you should spend a weekend going to as many sales as you can. These are generally listed in your local newspaper, usually under the heading "Garage Sales." Often times, people having a garage sale will post notices on the bulletin boards at their local market or grocery store. This is another good resource for you.

Don't forget all of these sources, because when you're ready to have your sale you'll want to advertise in some of them, too. However, if you live on a well-traveled road, all you may need is some signs pointing the way to have loads and loads of people stop to see what you've got for sale.

People like to barter when they attend yard and garage sales—that's part of the fun. A smart sales person (YOU) will mark and label EVERY-THING they intend to sell in a uniform and concise way. The price marked is usually a starting point for discussion. Clothes sell really cheaply (even expensive, well made items), so don't be surprised when you see beautiful suits and coats for ridiculously low prices. This is a great way to find good clothes to wear—but as a seller, you're not going to make much money reselling clothing. I've seen designer clothing sell for as little as $1.50, which, as I said before can be a real delight when you're shopping for a bargain— but a disappointment to the person trying to make money from the sale!

What are the types of things people will pay good money for? You will find people who are simply looking for cheap, cheap, cheap items for their own personal use. You will find individuals who are collectors scouting sales for something others have overlooked. You'll find college students, singles, and young professional couples trying to furnish their dorms, homes and apartments less expensively than they would if they shopped in regular stores. There is also a class of shopper you'll LOVE. These are people who just love to shop and spend money. They usually come early and try to buy everything interesting.

People are always looking for used appliances and furniture that are in good shape. If you have an old refrigerator, freezer, washer, dryer, etc., in good working condition, you can bet there is someone willing to pay you good money for it. Working color televisions and VCRs are very popular too! Air conditioners and dehumidifiers also sell really quickly at these types of sales. In other words, BIG TICKET ITEMS, which you can sell at a greatly reduced price and still make a good profit, will sell like hotcakes.

Antiques and collectibles are also very popular at "PERSONAL SURPLUS SALES." Again, perceived value plays a huge role. Unless you are a seasoned antique dealer, it's wise not to present furniture, crystal, silverware or other knickknacks as antiques unless you know this to be a fact. In most cases, you won't need to say a thing. People know what they're looking for and what pleases them. They may be more than willing to pay $150.00 for a table simply because they want it, not because you've claimed it to be Aunt Bessie's antique night stand. If you don't know the origin of a piece, always say so. People appreciate honesty. Besides, it's often such a rare commodity these days that this alone may help persuade them to buy from you.

On the other hand, if you have a piece which you know to be an antique, get it appraised before you try to sell it. It would be a shame to sell something worth thousands of dollars for a pittance! There was a segment on the Oprah Winfrey Show about a woman who sold some planters for a few hundred dollars only to find them in an antique store on sale for several thousand! OUCH!

Once you think you've seen enough yard and garage sales to try one of your own, it's time to gather the items you wish to sell in one place. Don't be afraid to ask friends and family to contribute if they have items they'd like to include. The bigger the sale, the better your chances of selling personal items!!

Remember, you'll want to price and mark the items clearly. You can simply use masking tape and a felt tip marker to do this—or purchase small self-adhering labels on which you can mark your prices. NEVER put the actual price you want on an item. Start high so the buyer can make you a lower offer which you can afford to accept, and the buyer will feel like he/she is getting a bargain. As I mentioned earlier, people love to feel like they got a deal.

Once you've got all of your merchandise labeled, you'll want to present it in a way that will attract the attention of people browsing through your sale. When possible, clothing should be hung on racks so it can be easily viewed. When you have items you are selling by the bunch (like books, records, children's clothes, etc.) try putting these in boxes which are labeled for the whole group. If you can sell a box of books for $5.00, when you might only sell 2 or 3 at a few cents each otherwise, it makes sense to put them together in a box to make the buyer feel they've found a bargain.

If you have small items which could easily be stolen, keep them close to where you will be perched. Unfortunately, there are shoplifters even at these types of sales. Which brings us to another point—money.

Make sure you stock up on change for the day of your sale. You won't believe how many people will hand you large bills for a purchase, expecting you to be able to make change. Prior to the sale you'll want to decide whether you will take checks. Some sales operate on a cash only basis. This is probably the safest bet—but you will have to make that determination yourself. It can be REALLY annoying to take a check from someone only to find out that it's no good. Since you're not a store, you won't want to be hassled with tracking someone down if they give you a bad check. Initially, you should just make it a policy to take cash only. Anyone really interested in buying from you will be able to comply.

PERSONAL SURPLUS SALES can be held simply to rid yourself of unnecessary or unwanted items—or they can be a method by which you can make extra income. For those of you looking for a way to make a living, the PERSONAL SURPLUS SALE can even provide you with this! A good example would be when you buy items from government auctions at 10 cents or less on the dollar and can then turn around and sell them for much, much more. The beauty of the PERSONAL SURPLUS SALE is that you decide just how far you want to take it.

Chapter 7:
County Sheriff Sales &
County/City Marshals
Auctions

> Hall of Fame baseball player Ernie Banks' sterling silver 50-ounce bat, his 500th home run ball and the 500th home run 4-foot high trophy sold at auction for $13,500, $14,000 and $13,000 respectively. Banks lost these items in a divorce settlement to his ex-wife. A Beverly Hills, CA firm conducted the auction. The Banks collection, which contained 85 items, brought in $82,000.

Believe it or not, sheriff's auctions date back to Feudal England, when the sheriff was the individual who foreclosed on a peasant for failing to pay his taxes. He then sold the merchandise at auction. Things really haven't changed that much over the years—have they?

In cities across the U.S. these sales are still conducted by a city or county marshal. Don't confuse them with the U.S. Marshals Service—county sheriff officers are part of local government and have nothing to do with the federal government. They repossess the property (most often vehicles like cars, trucks and jeeps) and then handle the auction themselves.

There is no set pattern, rhyme or even particular reason to when, where or how a sale will be conducted. However, these auctions are usually advertised in your local paper. Also, you can probably find out about upcoming auctions by calling your county sheriff, or city or county marshal. Don't be surprised if they are sometimes less than friendly—many won't welcome your call because they have so many other tasks which they feel are more important. **<u>DON'T GIVE UP!</u>** Be polite, but let them know it is your right to have this information.

You may want to send a self-addressed, stamped envelope with a letter asking the County Sheriff or County/City Marshals office to send you a flier for the next auction. Regardless of whether you are calling or writing, make it a point to ask if they maintain a mailing list for upcoming auctions. If they do—get on it!

Merchandise which comes up for auction by the county sheriff or local government marshal has most likely been repossessed. Once in a while they will have property which came from a drug bust. You may find business equipment which has been seized to satisfy a judgment.

You'll want to be sure not to purchase merchandise which has a lien on it. If you successfully bid on something only to find out that you own a lien, you won't be very happy. A lien is not an asset. When a buyer purchases property with a lien, he is responsible for paying the previous owner's debt. In order to avoid this you can take a trip to your county recorder's office and research the title. The county clerk or his/her assistants will assist you in doing a title search.

Sheriff sales are wonderful places for finding great bargains. How about a $100,000 home for only $15? Sound too good to be true? Well, it happened at a sheriffs sale. The quality of merchandise sold at these auctions varies greatly. The deals you can find are better than many you will find at the larger, more professionally run auctions.

On the following pages, we've provided contacts for County Sheriffs across the U.S., which should give you a good head start.

Best Bet Auctions

#1—The U.S. Trustees Bankruptcy Auctions offer great bargains and real steals. Because our court systems are so overworked, these auctions are a real gold mine. There's lots of information on these sales in Chapter 5.

Alabama

Mobile County Commissioners
P.O. Box 1448
Mobile, AL 36633
(334) 937-0264

Arizona

Sheriff of Maricopa
102 W. Madison
Phoenix, AZ 85003
(602) 256-1000
(602) 234-0517 (Vehicles)

Pima County Sheriff's Dept.
Civil Processing Unit
Court Information Section
P.O. Box 910
Tucson, AZ 85702
(602) 740-5510

California

Orange County Sheriff's Dept.
Orange County Register
11141 E. Chestnut
Santa Ana, CA 92705
(714) 583-9506

Orange County Sheriff
P.O. Box 449
Santa Ana, CA 92702
(714) 647-7000

Fresno County Sheriff's Dept.
Fresno County Bldg.
2200 Fresno Street
Fresno, CA 93724
(209) 488-3939

Los Angeles County Vehicles
Auction
2500 S. Garfield
City of Commerce, CA 90040
(213) 720-6952
(213) 720-6951 (Hotline)

Riverside County Garage
4293 Orange Street
Riverside, CA 92501
(714-275-6890 / 946-3386

Sacramento County
6670 Elvas Avenue
Sacramento, CA 95819
(916) 732-3841

Roger Ernst Assoc. Auctioneer
P.O. Box 3251
Modesto, CA 95353
(209) 527-7399

San Diego Public Admin. Office
5201-A Ruggin Road
San Diego, CA 92123
(619) 694-3500

San Francisco Sheriff's Dept.
Civil Division, 333 City Hall
Federal Bldg., Hall of Justice
San Francisco, CA 94102
(415) 554-7230

Santa Clara County
San Jose Sheriff's Dept.
Purchasing Dept.
1608 Las Plumas
San Jose, CA 91533
(707) 255-1404
(Nationwide vehicle)

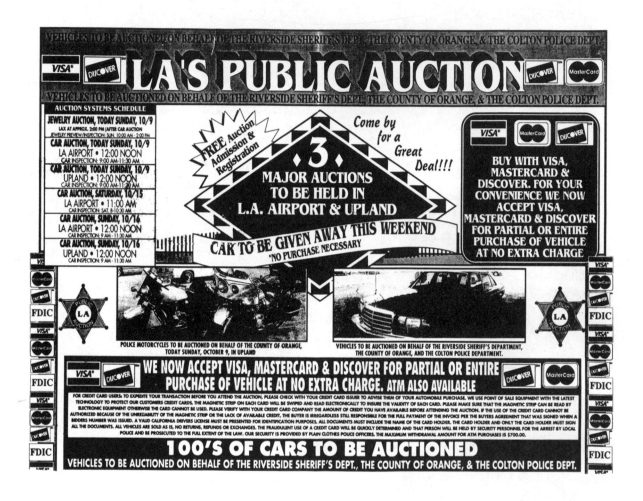

Colorado

Denver Sheriff's Dept.
Civil Division
City & County Bldg.
Denver, CO 80202
(303) 640-5192

Connecticut

Hartford County Sheriff's Dept.
P.O. Box 6302
Hartford, CT 06106
(203) 566-4930

Delaware

Newcastle County Sheriff's
Dept.
1020 King Street
Wilmington, DE 19801
(302) 571-7568

Florida

Duval County
Office of Sheriff
501 E. Bay Street
Jacksonville, FL 32202
(904) 630-0500

Metro Dade Police Dept.
Sheriff's Services
Civil Process Bureau, 13th Floor
Dade County Courthouse
Miami, FL 33130
(305) 595-6263

Orange County Sheriff's Dept.
P.O. Box 1440
Orlando, FL 32802
(407) 657-2500

Sarasota County Sheriff's Dept.
P.O. Box 4115
Sarasota, FL 34237
(813) 951-5800

Hillsborough County Sheriff's
Dept
Fiscal Division
P.O. Box 3371
Tampa, FL 33601
(813) 247-8031 / 247-8033

Palm Beach County Sheriff's
Dept.
3328 Gun Club Road
Palm Beach, FL 33406
(407) 688-3000

Georgia

Fulton County Sheriff
185 Central Avenue
Atlanta, GA 30303
(404) 730-5100

Hawaii

Honolulu County Sheriff's Dept.
2nd Floor, 111 Alakea Street
Honolulu, HI 96813
(808) 538-5665

Illinois

Cook County Sheriff's Office
Real Estate Division
50 W. Washington, Room 701-A
Chicago, IL 60602
(312) 443-3345 Personal
Property
(301) 443-3341 Real Estate

Sheriff's Department Auto
Pound
3145 S. Archer Avenue
Chicago, IL 60608
(312) 890-3355

Indiana

Allen County Sheriff's Dept.
Civil Division
Courthouse, Room 100
Fort Wayne, IN 46802
(219) 449-7632

Marion County Sheriff's Dept.
200 E. Washington, Room 822
Indianapolis, IN 46204
(317) 231-8415

Property Room
40 S. Alabama
Indianapolis, IN 46204
(317) 231-8294

Kentucky

Jefferson County Police
Garage
3528 Newburg Road
Louisville, KY 40218
(502) 452-2571
(812) 283-0734

Louisiana

E. Baton Rouge Parish
County Sheriff's Office
Foreclosure Dept., Room 229
P.O. Box 3277
Baton Rouge, LA 70821
(504) 389-4818

Orleans Parish
Civic Sheriff's Dept.
Moveable/Real Estate
421 Loyola Avenue
New Orleans, LA 70112
(504) 523-6143

Maryland

Baltimore City Sheriff's Office
100 N. Calvert Street, Room 104
Baltimore, MD 21202
(410) 396-5826

Massachusetts

Suffolk County Sheriff's Office
Civil Process Division
11 Beacon Street, Suite 910
Boston, MA 02108
Note: Refer to The Boston Herald's
Legal Section on Fridays.

Michigan

Washtenaw County Sheriff's
Dept.
2201 Hogback Road
Ann Arbor, MI 48105
(313) 971-3911

Wayne County Sheriff's Dept.
1231 St. Antoine
Detroit, MI 48226
(313) 494-3060
(313) 479-2500 Auto Salvage

Kent County Purchasing Dept.
Comptrollers Office
300 Monroe, NW
Grand Rapids, MI 49503
(616) 336-3500

Minnesota

Ramsey County Sheriff's Dept.
Civil 14 W. Kellogg Blvd.
St. Paul, MN 55102
(612) 266-9300

Missouri

St. Charles County Sheriff's
Dept.
301 N. Second
St. Charles, MO 63301
(314) 949- 0809 / 949-3010

Jackson County Sheriff's Dept.
Purchasing & Supply Division
City Hall Building
415 E. 12th, 7th Floor
Kansas City, MO 64106
(816) 881-3978

Sheriff's Dept. City of St. Louis
Civic Court Bldg.
10 N. Tucker
St. Louis, MO 63101
(314) 622-4851

Nebraska

Douglas County
Purchasing Dept., Room 902
Civic Center
Omaha, NE 68183
(402) 444-7158

Nevada

Clark County Sheriff's Civil
Bureau
310 S. 3rd Street, Suite 304
Las Vegas, NV 89155
(702) 455-4237

New Jersey

Mercer County Sheriff's Dept.
Box 8068
Trenton, NJ 08650
(609) 989-6100

New Mexico

Bernalillo County Sheriff's Dept.
Court Services Division
P.O. Box 1829
Albuquerque, NM 87103
(505) 768-4140

Ohio

Hamilton County Sheriff's Dept.
11021 Hamilton Avenue
Cincinnati, OH 45231
(513) 825-1500

Cuyahoga County Sheriff's
Dept.
1215 W. Third Street
Cleveland, OH 44113
(216) 443-6000

Franklin County Sheriff's Office
369 S. High Street
Columbus, OH 43215
(614) 462-3360

Montgomery County Purch.
Dept.
41 N. Perry Street
Dayton, OH 45422
(513) 255-6464 / 225-4357

Lucas County Court House
Clerk's Office
700 Adams & Erie Streets
Toledo, OH 43624
(419) 245-4000 / 245-4490

Mahoning County Sheriff's Dept.
Court Services Office
110 5th Ave.
Youngstown, OH   44503
(216) 740-2388

Oklahoma

Oklahoma County Sheriff's
Dept.
201 N. Shartel
Oklahoma City, OK 73102
(405) 236-1717

Tulsa County Sheriff's Dept.
500 S. Denver
Tulsa, OK 74103
(918) 596-5601

Oregon

Multnomah County Sheriff's
Dept.
12240 NE Glisan Street
Portland, OR 97230
(503) 255-3600 ext. 500 Hotline

Pennsylvania

Lehigh County Sheriff's Dept.
455 Hamilton St.
Allentown, PA 18101
(610) 820-3175

Philadelphia County Procedure
Surplus
Property Disposal Room 1330
15th & JFK Blvd.
Philadelphia, PA 19102
(215) 686-4765

Allegheny County Sheriff's Dept.
111 Courthouse, Grant St.
Pittsburgh, PA 19219
(412) 350-4704 / 350-4700

Luzern County Courthouse
200 North River Street
Wilkes Barre, PA 18711
(717) 825-1651

Rhode Island

Sheriff's Office of Providence
County
250 Benefit Street
Providence, RI 02903
(401) 277-3510

South Carolina

Charles County Sheriff's Office
3505 Pinehaven Dr.
Charleston Heights, SC 29405
(803) 554-4700

Pitt County Sheriff's Dept.
Main County Office Building
1717 W. Fifth Street
Greenville, SC 27834
(919) 830-6302 / 830-6306

Tennessee

Memphis Police Dept.
Property & Evidence Division
201 Poplar, Room LL106
Memphis, TN 38103
(901) 576-2550 Property
(901) 353-8200 Vehicles

Madison Sheriff's Dept.
506 Second Avenue N.
Nashville, TN 37201
(615) 862-8170

Texas

Travis County Sheriff's Dept.
P.O. Box 1748
Austin, TX 78767
(512) 322-4610 / 322-4615

Dallas County Sheriff's Dept.
133 N. Industrial Blvd.
Dallas, TX 75207
(214) 653-3500

El Paso County Sheriff's Dept.
800 E. Overland Street
El Paso, TX 79901
(915) 546-2217
(915) 858-3903 Vehicles

Harris County Sheriff's Dept.
1001 Prewston, Showroom 670
Houston, TX 77002
(713) 755-5036 Hotline

Bexar County Sheriff's Dept.
200 N. Comal
San Antonio, TX 78207
(210) 270-6000

Utah

Salt Lake County Sheriff's
Office
437 South 200 East
Salt Lake City, UT 84111
(801) 535-5441

Virginia

Richmond Sheriff's Dept.
400 N. 9th St., Suite LL1
Richmond, VA 23219
(804) 780-6600

Norfolk Sheriff's Dept.
P.O. Box 3908
Norfolk, VA 23514
(804) 785-7400

Washington

Dept. of Public Safety
King County Police
513 Third Avenue, Room W150
Seattle, WA 98104
(206) 296-3311

Wisconsin

Milwaukee County Sheriff's
Dept.
821 W. State Street
Milwaukee, WI 53233
(414) 278-4907

AUCTION #1 — JEWELRY, COINS, AND COLLECTIBLES
SATURDAY, OCTOBER 15, 1994 at 10:00 AM

ON BEHALF OF U.S. POSTAL INSPECTION, BURBANK P.D., STATE AND LOCAL LAW ENFORCEMENT AGENCIES & OTHERS

14K Heart Shape Diamond Pendent

14K Diamond/Ruby Bracelet

14K Diamond/Ruby Necklace

Plantinum Ring w/6½CT Solitaire Diamond

INVENTORY INCLUDES APPROXIMATELY 400 LOTS OF DIAMOND AND PRECIOUS STONE RINGS, PENDANTS, EARRINGS, NECKLACES, WATCHES, BRACELETS, SCRAP GOLD (INCLUDING A LARGE 14K GOLD AND DIAMOND MEDALLION. APPROX. 366 GNS TW & 6.55CT TDW), LOOSE STONES (INCLUDING A 1.01CT LOOSE ROUND BRILLANT DIAMOND), GOLD AND SILVER COINS, PAPER CURRENCY, CELLULAR PHONES, FAX MACHINES, SPORTS CARDS AND MEMORIBILIA. PLUS MANY MORE COLLECTIBLES TOO NUMEROUS TO LIST.

INSPECTION: FRIDAY, OCTOBER 15 FROM 10AM - 5PM AND MORNING OF SALE FROM 9AM ON.

TERMS OF SALE: 25% DEPOSIT IN CASH OR CASHIER'S CHECK IS REQUIRED ON AWARD OF BID. BALANCE IN CASH OR CASHIER'S CHECK

Chapter 8:
U.S. Postal Service Auctions

> "Last time I went to an auction there were 6 or 7 lots and one guy wanted them all, and wouldn't let anyone else get any. So he bid up the price. He could have paid $300 per lot, but he ended up paying twice that because he wouldn't let anyone else win any bids. You need to learn when to sit back and when to speak up!"
>
> J. Souza

People often leave town without a forwarding address, or packages are not labeled or wrapped properly, so all these parcels end up in the dead parcel branch of the postal service. Then guess what happens? These packages are gathered together for auction at five regional centers across the U.S. And this is where **YOU** enter the picture!

If you are lucky enough to live (or be visiting) one of the five cities where auctions are held — New York, Philadelphia, Atlanta, St. Paul and San Francisco — you may find just what you've been looking for at a postal service auction.

Auctions are held on a pretty regular basis in these areas. Each region maintains a mailing list, so as soon as you get on it, you'll be sent fliers letting you know about all of the upcoming auctions.

You're liable to find books, compact discs, videos, sporting goods and clothing at these auctions. An item frequently 'lost in the mail' is gifts. As a rule of thumb, if it was good enough for someone to send as a special present, it's good enough for you, too — especially if it costs you only 5 cents on the dollar!

All merchandise is sold in tubs, bins or lots. So you're bidding on all sorts of items at one time. The Postal Service tries to lump similar items together whenever possible.

When you attend vehicle sales you'll find jeeps, vans and trucks. Vehicles are sold whenever a surplus exists. It's hard for them to let you know when this will occur. Keep in close touch with several Post Offices, because from time to time you'll find some really exceptional deals on vehicles! Postal vehicle sales are usually advertised in local post offices and newspapers, and sometimes through television advertisements. Postal sales of excess computers, office furniture, and mail handling equipment are advertised in the same manner.

The inspection period for a Postal Service auction occurs about one to two hours prior to the start of the auction. When you register, you'll be given a paddle which will have your identification number on it.

Postal Service auctions are pretty cut and dried, and will generally go as follows:

1. The auctioneer will start the bidding with a minimum bid and make steady, rapid increases in small increments.

2. When you are interested in bidding, you hold your paddle in the air.

3. When the price is more than you wish to spend, you lower your paddle so the number is not showing.

4. The bidding ends when only one paddle is still in the air.

There are minimum bids at these auctions. Many times they are extremely low ($20 or $30 for a bin of merchandise). Postal Service auctions attract all sorts of people because the variety of items available are so diverse. Lots of people come to get bargains on books, tapes and CDs. People looking for unusual bargains at good prices know these auctions are worth attending.

Auctions usually last from 10:00 a.m. until 1:00 or 2:00 p.m. These are quick, high intensity events. Cash is preferred, although some accept money orders or cashier's checks.

Beginning on the following page is a listing of the various contacts you'll want to check for upcoming auctions. We have listed the five regions, plus the contacts for unclaimed merchandise auctions. You should also contact your local postmaster by looking in your telephone directory for U.S. Postal Service under the "U.S. Government" listings at the front of the phone book.

U.S. Postal Service Contacts

For information on personal property sales, write:

U.S. Postal Service
Material Support Operations Division
Office of Material Management
475 L'Enfant Plaza SW, Room 1021
Washington, DC 20260-6226

You may also contact the following program offices at the address listed for the state in which you are interested in buying property:

Alaska, Arizona, California, Hawaii, Idaho, Montana, New Mexico, Nevada, Oregon, Texas, Utah, Washington, and all Pacific Possessions and Trust Territories are covered by:

> **Manager, Material Management Branch**
> **Procurement and Material Management Service Center**
> **U.S. Postal Service**
> **850 Cherry Avenue**
> **San Bruno, CA 94099-6262**

District of Columbia, Delaware, Kentucky, Maryland, New Jersey, North Carolina, Ohio, South Carolina, Pennsylvania, Virginia, and West Virginia are covered by:

Manager, Material Management Branch
Procurement and Material Management Service Center
U.S. Postal Service
P.O. Box 8601
Philadelphia, PA 19197-6260

Connecticut, Maine, Massachusetts, New Hampshire, New Jersey, New York, Puerto Rico, Rhode Island, the Virgin Islands, and Vermont are covered by:

Manager, Material Management Branch
Procurement and Material Management Service Center
U.S. Postal Service
6 Griffin Center North
Windsor, CT 06006-6260

Colorado, Illinois, Indiana, Iowa, Kansas, Michigan, Minnesota, Missouri, Nebraska, South Dakota, Wisconsin, and Wyoming are covered by:

Manager, Material Management Branch
Procurement and Material Management Service Center
U.S. Postal Service
433 West Van Buren Street
Chicago, IL 60699-6260

Alabama, Arkansas, Florida, Georgia, Louisiana, Mississippi, Oklahoma, and Tennessee are covered by:

Manager, Material Management Branch
Procurement and Material Management Service Center
U.S. Postal Service
1407 Union Avenue
Memphis, TN 38166-6260

For information on unclaimed merchandise "dead letter" auctions, write to the office where you are interested in attending sales:

Superintendent
USPS
Undeliverable Mail
1970 Market Street, Room 531A
Philadelphia, PA 19104-9651

Superintendent
USPS
Claims & Inquiry and Undeliverable Mails
1300 Evans Avenue
San Francisco, CA 94188-9661

Manager
USPS
Dead Parcel Branch
J.A. Farley Bldg., Room 2029-A
New York, NY 10099-9599

Supervisor
USPS
Undeliverable Mails
180 East Kellog Blvd., Room 932
St. Paul, MN 55101-9514

Supervisor
USPS
Undeliverable Mails
730 Great Southwest Parkway
Atlanta, GA 30336-9590

Greedy spy's loot to be sold at auction

The tri-color gold wedding band is the cheapest of the lot.

By BRIGID SCHULTE
KNIGHT-RIDDER NEWS SERVICE

WASHINGTON — Driven by greed, CIA spy Aldrich Ames sold his soul, his country and the lives of as many as 11 agents to the KGB for $2.5 million. This week, the U.S. government will begin to get a little of its own back.

More than $100,000 worth of Aldrich and Rosario Ames' Rolex and Cartier watches, elegant white gold and sapphire earrings, Gucci purses with the coins still in them,

Tiffany boxes, and a mess of costume jewelry — confiscated trappings of the convicted spy's once-luxurious lifestyle — will go to the highest bidder at a public auction Thursday

Ames

in Atlanta.

"We have had an unbelievable amount of interest," said Mark Clifford of Manheim Auctions, which will sell the loot. "Your kids may read about this traitor in history books in high school, and you could say, 'Well, I have his Rolex.'"

Dean Echols, Manheim's director of government services, said, "Some of it appears to be gifts from foreign agents."

The auction house has a five-year contract with the U.S. Marshals Service to sell all collectibles seized by federal officials in drug raids, tax forfeitures and, now, espionage cases east of the Mississippi. The money earned from the Ames collection is to go to a fund to help victims of violent crimes.

Rosario Ames, who pleaded guilty to espionage and tax evasion and is serving a five-year sentence, said at her trial that she did not know her husband was selling U.S. secrets to the Soviets and their Russian successors until 1992. She thought the cash that went to pay for their $540,000 house, $40,000 Jaguar and astronomical monthly credit-card bills came from investments her husband made with a man he called "Roger from Chicago."

Rosario Ames said that when she discovered his secret, her husband manipulated her. She accused him of "the worst form of spousal abuse." Apparently that didn't stop her husband from showering her with jewels.

The sheer volume of booty to be sold — mostly women's jewelry — is astounding: 16 necklaces of pearl, gold, crystal and opal; 17 pairs of diamond earrings, 12 gold and jeweled bracelets, chokers, pendants, a silver pillbox with "Rosarito" engraved on it, seven long gold chains, eight watches; and 14 rings in emerald, sapphire, diamond or pearl. The tri-color gold wedding band is the cheapest of the lot.

Other items include a glass fish, a Swiss army knife, an 18-karat-gold fountain pen and a "gold inlay plexiglass artifact" — not quite as garish as the diamond Jesus pendant and panther ring to be auctioned at the same time from a seized drug dealer's estate.

As for the rest of the Ameses' worldly possessions, the FBI has decided not to sell the $40,000 red Jaguar. The computer with the stored information that clinched the government's case against Ames is now in government use — minus the damning disks.

The Ameses' Kitchen Aid Mixmaster, Cuisinart, stereo, bread maker and Krups espresso machine go on the block in Springfield, Va., next month in a separate government auction. And the gray Colonial house with a leaking basement, now going for $470,000, still sits on the market.

Chapter 9:
U.S. Marshals Service

"Over the years, my wife and I have bought hundreds of items at auctions. I used to own an art gallery in Taos, New Mexico, which is how I became involved in the auction process to start with. I began going to art auctions and before I knew it, I was hooked! Then I began to see how much money we could save on everyday items, so we would scour auctions, garage sales, swap meets, etc. I've purchased many items at rock bottom prices and turned around and sold them for several hundred, even thousands of dollars."

D. Rutledge

The U.S. Marshals Service is a branch of the U.S. Justice Department. In the mid-1970's when the National Asset Seizure and Forfeiture Program went into effect, the U.S. Marshals Service was given the task of managing and selling the seized assets of administrative or judicial forfeiture. As the drug trade has flourished and the DEA and FBI started busting big time crooks, drug dealers and even members of drug cartels, the Marshals Service has been pushed into the auction business with a vengeance!

Yes, it was a Marshals Service auction which sold a $50,000 boat for $10. The Marshals Service sales are where you are highly likely to find the vehicles, boats, airplanes and other luxury items associated with the drug trade.

The vehicles, merchandise and other items you'll find at a Marshal's Service auction come primarily from drug busts. Add to this the luxury items confiscated when a white collar crime is committed, and you have the makings for a GREAT auction. <u>**Generally, the DEA and FBI contribute the largest amount of goods to an auction.**</u>

Marshals Service auctions operate with a reserve price. Since they are not professional appraisers, items are often mispriced. This can be a real advantage for you if something is worth $10,000 and they are willing to sell it for $5,500!

Probably the most difficult task you'll have with regards to Marshals Service auctions is finding out when and where they will be held. This, however, can be a big benefit in cutting down on your competition. The auctions are decentralized, which means that each office operates their program individually from 49 separate districts.

Fortunately, they sometimes give their merchandise over to the GSA who then handles it for them. But it is not uncommon for the Marshals Service to hire private auctioneers or to sell the property themselves using their own staff to perform the auction.

There are two types of assets handled by the Marshals Service: criminal and civil. Both come to auction at some point in time. Civil assets consist of the profits of criminal activity. Drug lords are known to launder their cash through restaurants, leasing companies, retail outlets, etc. The Marshals Service is supposed to keep these businesses running profitably so they can be sold. Since they are not known for being too good at managing any of these businesses, you can often pick up an entire business for a song.

Criminal assets are what has been confiscated when a crime is actually being committed. This is where the big money, fast boats, expensive cars, airplanes and the like come into play. These are not released as quickly as civil assets because they are often used during the trial as evidence.

The U.S. Marshals Service advertises their confiscated goods in *USA Today* on Wednesdays. You may want to go down to your local newsstand and pick up a copy of the *USA Today* next Wednesday so you can look at a current copy. The ad shows property and merchandise which has been confiscated. Again, because some of this property will be used as evidence during a trial, not all of it will be available immediately, but by looking at these advertisements you'll be able to get a pretty good idea of the types of things for sale.

The U.S. Marshals Service now has an electronic bulletin board system for those of you with a computer and modem. You can contact it by dialing 1-202-208-7679. They have gathered quite a bit of valuable information together on this BBS system which will be highly useful to you. For those of you without a computer and modem, we have provided information for your use as well following this chapter.

The following list is of contract service providers and Federal agencies who are currently authorized by the U.S. Marshals Service to sell forfeited property on a regular basis. This list provides information on company or agency names, telephone numbers and locations. You can contact the companies listed to obtain information on the property that is currently available as well as sales locations and dates.

Please note that if you contact any of these companies/agencies by mail you must include a <u>self-addressed, stamped envelope.</u> This should be a #10 legal size envelope with your name and address printed NEATLY on it. Also, when contacting any agency, please do not call collect. They are not able to accept collect calls.

In addition to the company / agency list we have provided, you should look in your telephone book.   To learn more about the U.S. Marshals Service program, they would be listed under the Department of Justice under the main heading of the "U.S. Government" in your phone book. If you live in a small town and there is no listing, you may want to call your public library and ask them to look up the telephone numbers for the major cities in your state.

For information write:

U.S. Marshals Service
National Seized Assets Forfeiture Service
600 Army Navy Drive
Arlington, VA 22202-4210

United States Marshals Service
National Sellers List

ALABAMA

Acton & Associates, Birmingham (205) 823-2330

Real Estate:
Target Auction & Land Co., Inc., Bessemer (205) 425-5454

Arizona

Motor Vehicles:
Gary's Towing, Tucson (520) 574-9161
Thompson Towing & Salvage, Yuma (602) 726-5561

Real Estate:
Blue Chip Properties, Phoenix (602) 234-0517

California

Motor Vehicles:
ABRE Enterprises Inc., San Diego (619) 661-1955
Nationwide Companies, Los Angeles (818) 968-3110
Nationwide, Northern California (707) 255-1766
Dunham Diversified Services, El Centro (619) 375-5858, Hotline (619) 353-1319

TO BE SOLD ON BEHALF OF THE UNITED STATES MARSHALS SERVICE

1993 DUCATI 900SL MOTORCYCLE	1988 FORD BRONCO	1985 PORSCHE 944
1992 LEXUS SC400	1988 MERCURY COUGAR ZR-7	1984 BMW 528E
1992 NISSAN MAXIMA	1987 MERCURY COUGAR	1981 HARLEY DAVIDSON MOTORCYCLE
1989 CHEVROLET CORVETTE CONVERTIBLE	1987 SOONER-DUNCAN HORSE TRAILER	1978 LINCOLN MARK V
1989 MERCEDES BENZ 300E	1986 PORSCHE	1975 GMC MOTORHOME
1989 BMW M3	1984 CHEVROLET MONTE CARLO	1972 PANTERA
1989 JEEP CHEROKEE	1984 KENWORTH TRUCK TRACTOR CONV.	1969 CHEVROLET CORVETTE
1989 FORD CROWN VICTORIA		1967 ROLLS ROYCE

Real Estate:
Prudential Realty, Santa Rosa (707) 528-7653, 1-800-773-8767
Los Feliz, Los Angeles (213) 662-3157
South Coast Equities, San Diego (619) 291-8780
U.S. GSA, San Francisco 1-800-676-SALE

Colorado

Denver (303) 844-2801
(Dickensheet & Associates (303) 934-8322)

Connecticut

Motor Vehicles:
U.S. General Services Admin. (GSA), Waltham, MA (617) 565-7326
 (recorded message)

Real Estate:
Heritage Asset Management, Hartford (203) 728-1776

Delaware

Real Estate:
Town & Country Properties, Inc., Fairfax, VA (703) 698-4811, 698-4950

District of Columbia

Real Estate:
Town & Country Properties, Inc., Fairfax, VA (703) 698-4811, 698-4950

Florida

Motor Vehicles and Vessels:
U.S. General Services Admin. (GSA), Kennedy Space Center
 (407) 867-7637 (recorded message)
 Jim Gall Auctioneers, Inc. (305) 573-1616

Real Estate:
Prudential Florida, Tampa (813) 441-2807, 442-4111
ICF Kaiser Engineers, Miami (305) 777-5217
U.S. General Services Admin. (GSA), Atlanta (404) 331-5133
 (recorded message)

Georgia

Motor Vehicles:
Bishop Brothers Auto Auction, Atlanta (404) 767-3652
Savannah Auto Auction, Savannah (912) 965-0616
Cassidy's Garage, Macon (912) 742-3832

Real Estate:
U.S. General Services Admin. (GSA), Atlanta (404) 331-5133
 (recorded message)
Century 21 Sea Mar, Douglas (912) 384-0316
Golden Isles Realty Co., St. Simons (912) 638-8623
USMS, Atlanta Area (recorded message) (404) 730-9252

Personal Property:
Manheim Auctions (800) 222-9885
Harris Auction Service, Fairburn (404)969-1315

Hawaii

Motor Vehicles & Real Estate:
U.S. General Services Admin. (GSA), Hawaii (808) 541-1972

Illinois

Marshal's Auction Hotline: (312) 353-0101

Motor Vehicles:
Fab Transit, Inc. Chicago (773) 927-0620
Giganti Properties, Springfield (217) 793-3300

Real Estate:
CS&R Checkmate, Chicago (312) 609-9744

Indiana

Motor Vehicles:
Kesler-Schaefer Auto Auction, Indianapolis (317) 297-2300

Kansas

Motor Vehicles:
(GSA) U.S. General Services Admin., Kansas City

Kentucky

Motor Vehicles:
Auto Dealers Exchange, Lexington (606) 263-5163
Parkers Commercial Storage, Louisville (502) 636-5817

Real Estate:
Dick Vreeland & Assoc., Louisville (502) 636-5817

Electronic Equipment:
Dick Vreeland & Assoc., Louisville (502) 636-5817

Louisiana

Motor Vehicles:
Gallagher Transfer & Storage Co., New Orleans (504) 943-2000
Pedersen & Pedersen Auction, Dry Creek (318) 494-1333

Hemphill & Assoc., Baton Rouge (504) 272-9635

Personal Property:
Hemphill & Assoc., Baton Rouge (504) 928-1144

Maryland

Motor Vehicles:
Parkville Automotive, Inc., Baltimore (410) 668-6600

Real Estate:
Town & Country Properties, Inc., Fairfax, VA (7030 698-4811, 698-4950

Massachusetts

Motor Vehicles:
U.S. General Services Admin. (GSA), Waltham, MA (617) 565-7326
(recorded message)

Michigan

Motor Vehicles:
M&M Inc., Grand Rapids (616) 776-0264
Auto Pool Auction, Romulus, MI (313) 479-4360

Advest Realty (810) 559-3333
NE Property Management (810) 771-7100

Montana

Motor Vehicles:
Berry's Automotive Service, Helena (406) 458-9210

Nevada

Motor Vehicles:
Liberty Auctions, Las Vegas (702) 871-4693
Stremmel Auctions, Reno (702) 329-1300

Personal Property:
Stremmel Auctions, Reno (702) 329-1300
Liberty Auctions, Las Vegas (702) 871-4693

New Hampshire

Motor Vehicles:
GSA, Waltham (recorded message) (617) 565-7326

New Jersey

Motor Vehicles:
U.S. General Services Admin. (GSA), Edison (908) 906-5609
(recorded message)
Swartz Auctioneers, Dover (201) 328-8310

New Mexico

Electronics:
Charles Dickerson Auction, Inc., Fairacres (505) 526-1106

SPECIAL AUCTION ON BEHALF OF THE UNITED STATES MARSHAL'S SERVICE

OCTOBER 16, 1994 AT 3:00PM THE FOLLOWING AIRCRAFT WILL BE SOLD AT UNITED BEECHRAFT, 2161 EAST AVION ST., ONTARIO INTERNATIONAL AIRPORT, ONTARIO, CA 91761

INSPECTION: THUR.-SAT., OCTOBER 13-15 AND SUN., OCTOBER 16 UNTIL AUCTION TIME. CONTACT ARMANDO CAMARENA AT THE NATIONWIDE COMPANIES FOR FURTHER INFO. (818) 968-3110.

1966 BOEING 727-100 AIRLINER N299LA, SERIAL NO. 19121

U.S. Marshals Service

JEWELRY AUCTION

OVER 300 LOTS! INCLUDING THIRTEEN ROLEX WATCHES, GOLD COINS, OVER 250 PIECES OF DIAMOND JEWELRY (UP TO 12.7 cts TDW), LOOSE GEMS, GOLD JEWELRY, BULLION AND RARE NUMISMATIC COINS, FINE ART, STAMPS AND MUCH MORE!

WHEN: **AUCTION 1 PM FRIDAY, OCTOBER 28**   **PREVIEW 10 AM TO 1 PM**
WHERE: **TARRANT COUNTY CONVENTION CENTER**   **FORT WORTH, TEXAS**
SALES TAX: Texas sales tax will be collected from buyers who are not buying for resale.
PAYMENT: In full immediately upon completion of auction by cash, cashier's check, or check with original bank letter of guarantee to Lone Star Auctioneers. Bank letters must read: "_____ is a customer of this bank. This bank will guarantee unqualified payment on account #_____, up to $_____.
2.5% fee will be added to checks without this fee. NO EXCEPTIONS!
AFFIDAVITS: Each bidder will be required to execute an affirmation that he/she is not, nor does he/she represent the individual(s) from whom property in the auction was seized.
TERMS: • "AS IS, WHERE IS" • NO WARRANTIES • NO GUARANTEES • NO REFUNDS • ALL SALES FINAL •
CATALOGS: Available at preview and auction.   **TRAVEL ARRANGEMENTS:** BRENHAM TRAVEL
ANNOUNCEMENTS MADE AUCTION DAY SUPERSEDE ALL PRIOR ADVERTISING

Motor Vehicles & Household:
Charles Dickerson Auction, Inc., Fairacres (505) 526-1106

Real Estate:
Voris & Assoc., Albuquerque (505) 275-8955

New York

Motor Vehicles:
U.S. Affiliates, Inc., New York (212) **252-3056**
Clinton Terminals, Inc., Plattsburg (518) 298-8052
Kvell, Inc., Buffalo (716) 873-9888
Cash Realty & Auctions, Buffalo (716) 633-2274
Great Arrow Storage, Buffalo (716) 874-1101 EXT. #2.

Personal Property:
Cash Realty & Auctions, Buffalo (716) 633-2274

North Carolina

Motor Vehicles:
Advance Business Service, Charlotte (704) 393-7335
DGS Contract Services, Inc., Charlotte (910) 897-4605
Mendenhall Auto Auction, High Point (910) 889-5700

Real Estate:
McCullen Realty, Clinton (910) 592-3703
Iron Horse Auction Co., Rockingham (910) 997-2248
Tarheel Auction & Realty, Statesville (704) 872-5800, 871-8770
Willie Gibson, Coldwell Banker Security Real Estate,
 Concord 1-800-992-9870

Personal Property; Electronic Equipment; Business Inventory:
John Pait & Assoc., Greensboro (910) 299-1186

Ohio

Motor Vehicles:
Cassell & Assoc., Worthington (614) 433-7355

Heritage Realtors, Dayton (513) 434-7600
Brookmeyer & Assoc., Dublin (614) 761-0021
Joe Walker & Assoc., Columbus (614) 891-0180

Oklahoma

Real Estate; Unique Motor Vehicles:
Williams & Williams, Tulsa (918) 250-2012

Pennsylvania

Motor Vehicles:
Vilsmeier Auction Co., Inc., Montgomeryville (215) 628-2303
U.S. General Services Admin. (GSA), Harrisburg (215) 656-3939
Flying Carport, Philadelphia (215) 492-1161

Real Estate:
Philadelphia Property Management, Philadelphia (215) 335-2900
Prudential Realty, Pittsburgh (412) 471-3200
Management Enterprises, Scranton (717) 346-4649

Puerto Rico

Motor Vehicles:
Manual Fuentes Reyes, Bayaman (809) 787-1932

Real Estate:
S.P. Management Corp., Rio Predras, San Juan (809) 758-6415,
 (809) 764-7474

Rhode Island

Motor Vehicles:
U.S. General Services Admin. (GSA), Waltham, MA (617) 565-7326
 (recorded message)

Real Estate:
Cameron & Lillibridge Realtors, East Greenwich (401) 885-5400

South Carolina

Real Estate:
U.S. General Services Admin.(GSA), Atlanta, GA (404) 331-5133
 (recorded message)

Tennessee

Motor Vehicles:
United Auto Recovery, Memphis (901) 795-5044

Texas

Motor Vehicles:
Abrego Trucking Service, Mc Allen (210) 631-4601
Hector Cabello Wrecker Service, Laredo (210) 723-2552
Robertson Leasing Corp., Del Rio (210) 775-7587, 775-9698
Gaston & Sheehan Auctioneers, Inc., Pflugerville, San Antonio,
 Austin-Waco (512) 251-2780, 251-3002
 Lone Star Auctioneers, (817) 740-9400 or (800) 275-3336
(Lone Star Auction does Marshal auctions for all of Texas)
Real Estate:
Urban Systems, San Antonio (512) 227-9435
Personal Property:
Lone Star Auctioneers, Inc. (817) 921-3336

Vermont

Motor Vehicles; Personal Property:
Thomas Hirchak Co., Morrisville 1-800-634-7653

Virginia

Motor Vehicles:
Star City Auto Auctions, Inc., Roanoke (703) 342-2700
Buchanan Auto Auction, Chesapeake (804) 485-3342
U.S. General Services Admin. (GSA), Franconia (703) 557-7785
recorded message at (703) 557-7796
Real Estate:
Town & Country Properties, Inc., Falls Church (703) 536-7650

Washington

Motor Vehicles:
James G. Murphy, Inc., Kenmore 1-800-426-3008

West Virginia

Motor Vehicles: (304) 623-5486

Wisconsin

Motor Vehicles:
(414) 297-1919 (Marshal's Office Auction Hotline)

State of Washington
Public Auction
Saturday, Sept 24, 1994 - 10:00 a.m.
Commodity Redistribution Yard
Warehouse 5 - C Street S.W. - Auburn

Cars

8 Cylinder Sedans

1	1991 Caprice
21	1988-1990 Caprice
4	1986-1989 Crown Vic
2	1989-1990 Mustang
1	1985 Pontiac Parisienne

6 Cylinder Sedans

1	1990 Taurus
6	1988-1989 Celebrity
8	1982-1983 Fairmont

4 Cylinder Sedans

7	1986-89 Aries/Reliant
4	1988-1989 Celebrity
2	1989 Escort
6	1986-88 Omni-Horizon

Trucks/Vans/4x4s

Pickups

15	1972 -1988 Models Chev,Datsun,Dodge, Ford,GMC,Mazda, Toyota

Vans

6	1977-1983 Models Chev,Dodge

4 x 4

5	1990 Pathfinder
11	1988-1989 Cherokee
5	1989-1990 Blazer
1	1988 Ramcharger
1	1988 Dodge Pickup
1	1987 Chev Pickup
1	1985 GMC Pickup
1	1985 S-10 Pickup
1	1983 S-10 Pickup

Quantities subject to change

1978 - 21' Boston Whaler , w/trailer,200HP Johnson, & 35HP Evinrude

Bidding

You may register to bid on Friday, Sept 23, from 8 am. to 4 pm. and from 8 am. on the day of the sale.
You will be assigned a bid number when you register.
Catalogs are available Friday, Sept 23 and Saturday, Sept 24, at the auction site.
You may inspect auction items on Sept 23, from 8 a.m. to 4 p.m. and from 8 a.m. until they are sold on the day of the sale.

Payments

You may pay for your purchase with cash, cashiers check, money order, or travelers checks.
Personal Checks only can be accepted when accompanied by a letter from your bank stating that: *The account of (customer's name) is in good standing and we will guarantee (or honor) checks presented to us by Oct.12,1994, up to the amount of (dollar amount) for the purchase of State of Washington property.*
A $100 holding fee is required on each vehicle until full payment is received.
If you do not have a resale number, sales tax will be collected on non-titled items.
All items must be paid for and removed by Wednesday, Sept. 28,1994.

STATE OF WISCONSIN VEHICLE AUCTION
OCTOBER 22 1994 - ARLINGTON

Chapter 10:
State Surplus Auctions

> Cherubini once granted an audition to a man possessed of a very powerful voice. Asked for a demonstration of his talents, he sang so forcefully that the window panes rattled. "Do you think anything can be made of me?" he asked Cherubini at the conclusion. "Certainly," was the reply. "An auctioneer."
>
> Maria Luigi Cherubini (1760-1842)

Just about every state conducts surplus auctions. State governments have an enormous amount of personal property and equipment for sale. If you are looking for bargains on used cars, this is a VERY good place to start! Just about every state auctions off the fleet vehicles used by government employees, as well as automobiles, vans, trucks, pick-ups, motorcycles, boats, etc., which have been confiscated by various state agencies. It's not unheard of for cars to go for $75 or even less.

This is an area of tremendous growth in most states, since the monies derived from auction help the state's coffers. States are quick to sell their used vehicles to buy new models, which can mean tremendous bargains for you! You have a better than average opportunity to buy a very good car at a great price when you attend state auctions!

The number of vehicles fluctuates from state to state. Some may have as few as a dozen to sell, while another state may have over 200 cars, trucks, and vans to dispose of.

On an average, state surplus auctions take place about once every three months. The average price for a car sold at state auction is around $900. MANY sell for less than $450 — which isn't too bad for a car that's <u>only two or three years old!</u>

It's not unusual for state surplus agencies to sell state university property at their auctions. State universities are the beneficiaries of major corporations which donate research equipment, computers, printing equipment, etc. The university uses this equipment for a couple of years and then sells it off. When you are contacting state offices to find out about auctions, be sure to ask them who handles the state university auctions for their state. Huge bargains can be found at these auctions!

Each state has its own rules and regulations with regard to when and where auctions are held, how they are handled, how they are advertised, etc. Your best bet is to contact the state listings which interest you so you can get on their mailing list. While not every state maintains a list, we have found the individuals running these programs to be VERY friendly and helpful. If they don't maintain a mailing list, they will tell you how you can find out about upcoming auctions.

One of the great benefits of state surplus auctions is not only their bargains, but the opportunity they provide you to hone your auction skills right in your own back yard, so to speak. And, of course you can also travel from state to state finding loads of good deals, regardless of where you live.

Nationwide State Auction & Surplus Contacts

Alabama

Alabama Surplus Property
P.O. Box 210487
Montgomery, AL 36121
(205) 277-5866

Alabama auctions off a variety of items about three times per year, including office equipment, heavy machinery (such as milling machines and drill presses), and vehicles, including cars, trucks, boats, and tractors. Trailers, medical equipment, tires, dossiers, and lathes are also sold. The state advertises upcoming auctions in local newspapers, but you can also be put on a mailing list. Payment can be by cash, cashier's check, or personal check with a bank letter of credit. Items are available for viewing two days prior to the auction. No bids by mail.

Alaska

Office of Surplus Property
2400 Viking Drive
Anchorage, AK 99501
(907) 465-2172

Alaska's Division of General Services and Supply sells surplus office equipment, including furniture and typewriters, every Tuesday from 8:30 a.m. to 12:00 p.m., and from 1:30 p.m. to 4:00 p.m. in a garage sale fashion with prices marked for each item. For items costing over $100, cash or cashiers checks are required. Vehicles are sold during sealed bid auctions at various locations throughout the state twice a year (in the spring and fall). Payment is by cashiers check once you've been notified of your winning bid.

Arizona

Office of Surplus Property
1537 W. Jackson Street
Phoenix, AZ 85007
(602) 542-5701

About four times each year Arizona auctions off everything from vehicles to miscellaneous office equipment and computers. Items are sold by lots rather than individually. Cars are often sold well below Blue Book price. Vehicles range from empty frames to Jaguars. A mailing list is maintained. Individual cities and counties in Arizona also hold their own surplus auctions.

Arkansas

State Marketing and Redistribution Office
6620 Young Road
Little Rock, AR 72201
(501) 565-8645

Arkansas conducts both bid and retail, fixed-price sales of surplus items. On Wednesdays between 7:30 a.m. and 3:00 p.m. buyers may view and purchase items which include everything from office machines, tables, and tires (valued at under $300) to larger, more valuable items such as vehicles, medical equipment, mobile homes, and machine shop and automotive supplies. In order to keep your name on the mailing list you must bid a minimum of three times. The state also conducts sealed bids by mail.

California

State of California
Office of Fleet Administration
1416 10th Street
Sacramento, CA 95814
(916) 327-2085
(916) 327-9196 (Hotline)

California sells surplus office equipment or other supplies only to schools and other non-profit or educational institutions. Once a month the General Services Department of the state holds auctions at the Sacramento or Los Angeles State Garages of surplus automobiles. Vehicles may include sedans, cargo and passenger vans, and pick-ups. Viewing is available prior to the auction. You can receive 2 weeks advance notice by getting on the mailing list. Payment is by cash, cashiers check, or certified check. Personal checks are also accepted, but items may not be picked up until the check has cleared the bank. No out of state checks are taken. Prices vary greatly.

California Highway Patrol
Used Vehicle Sales Office
3300 Reed Avenue
West Sacramento, CA 95605
(916) 371-2284 (Hotline)

The CHP auctions off vehicles such as Crown Victorias, Chevy Capris, Dodge Diplomats, 4x4s, Mustangs, and many more. Most have air conditioning, power steering, and power brakes. Minimum bids are stated on a recorded telephone message. The auction is by sealed bids which are opened at 3:00 p.m. daily. Winners may be notified by telephone. Payment is by cashiers check, certified check, or money order only. Inspection is available between 8:00 a.m. and 4:00 p.m.

Colorado

State Surplus Sales
4200 Garfield St.
Denver, Co 80216
(303) 321-4012

The state holds sales on a daily basis in a store-like setting between noon and 3:45 p.m. Items vary from day to day. Vehicles are auctioned separately several times a year. Advance notice is given in the newspaper. The car auctions are usually held on the second Saturday of the month. Vehicles customarily available include Ford LTDs, Plymouth Horizons, and Chevrolet Chevettes. Viewing is available one hour prior to the auction. Buyers may also purchase a brochure with vehicle descriptions for $3.00 on the day of the auction.

Connecticut

State Surplus Sales
60 State Street, Rear
Wethersfield, CT 06109
(203) 566-7018 or (203) 566-7190

Eight or nine times a year, the state advertises its auctions in the largest newspapers and on local radio. Unfortunately, there is no mailing list but the auctions are usually held the second Saturday of the month. You may preview one hour prior to the auction.

Delaware

Division of Purchasing
P.O. Box 299
Delaware City, DE 19706
(302) 834-4550

About two times each year Delaware publicly auctions off vehicles, office furniture and other surplus or used property. Vehicles include sedans, vans, pick-ups,school buses, and paddle boats. Prices depend on the condition of the item and how many people are bidding for it. Vehicles may be inspected and started up prior to the auction, but may not be driven. If you send a letter to the above address, they will put you on the mailing list so that you can be notified of upcoming auctions.

District of Columbia

The District of Columbia Dept. of Public Works
5001 Shepard Parkway S.W.
Washington, D.C. 20032
(202) 645-4227 or
(202) 645-5800

DC holds vehicle auctions on the first and third Tuesday of the month at 8:00 a.m. at Blue Plains. Vehicles include cars, trucks, buses, ambulances and boats. Inspection and viewing is available one hour prior to the auction. Prices and conditions of vehicles vary greatly. No mailing list is maintained.

District of Columbia Office of Property Control
2250 Shannon Place SE
Washington, D.C. 20032
(202) 645-0130

Three times per year this office auctions off items which include clothing, typewriters, cabinets, tools, refrigerators, and more at the DC Police Training Academy. No mailing list is kept, but advance notices are placed in the Washington Post. Viewing of items is allowed the day of the sale. Cash only is accepted.

Florida

The Bureau of Motor Vehicles and Water Craft
813 B Lake Bradford Rd.
Tallahassee, FL 32304
(904) 488-5177 / (800) 766-9266

Sells surplus items, including cars and boats. Automobile auctions take place anywhere from 8 to 10 times each year, with dates set 4 to 6 weeks in advance at various auction locations throughout the state. Industrial equipment is also included, along with various kinds of used and confiscated vans, trucks, cars and Blazers. Boats are auctioned twice a year and include pleasure and fishing boats. Items may be viewed two days prior to the auction (between 9:00 a.m. and 4:00 p.m. Friday; 8:00 a.m. to 10:00 a.m. Saturday). The auction begins at 10:00 a.m. on Saturday. A mailing list is maintained and you can be included by contacted MVW.

Georgia

State of Georgia
Department of Administrative Services, Purchasing Division
Surplus Property Services
1050 Murphy Avenue, SW
Atlanta, GA 30310
(404) 756-4800

Georgia auctions off vehicles, which include sedans, wagons, trucks, vans, buses and cement mixers. They also sell shop equipment, generators, typewriters, copiers, computers, tape recorders, other office equipment, as well as audio-visual equipment, cameras, electronic equipment, and air conditioners. A mailing list is maintained and sales are also advertised in local newspapers. Merchandise may be inspected two days before an auction. Auctions are held on the third Wednesday of a month if enough items have accumulated to warrant a sale. Vehicles may be started up but not driven. Sealed bids are also used and deposits are required with these. For auctions, items are purchased with cash or check with sufficient I.D. as long as the amount is under $500.00. For personal or business checks in amounts greater than $501.00 the property is held until the check has cleared the bank.

Hawaii

Hawaii does not presently conduct surplus sales at the state level.

Idaho

Bureau of Supplies
801 Reserve Street
Boise, ID 83712
(208) 377-6633

Every year the Bureau of Supplies auctions off surplus items including cars, equipment, televisions, chairs, office equipment, desks and typewriters. Items are sold individually. Local checks are accepted as payment with two I.D.'s. The Bureau maintains a mailing list and also advertises auctions in the local papers.

Illinois

Central Management Services
Division of Property Control
3550 Great Northern Avenue
Springfield, IL 62707
(217) 782-7786 or (217) 785-6903

Illinois has a program in which the public can purchase surplus personal property. It is state property that has been used to its life expectancy or property that must be replaced for safety or economic reasons. Also included are items that are obsolete or in excess of the state's needs. Numerous items are available including operable and inoperable vehicles, office equipment, electronic data processing equipment, laboratory equipment, and scrap metal. Usable surplus property is sold at regular intervals by public auction at the State Surplus Property Warehouse located at 1912 S. 10-1/2 Street, Springfield. Auction/bid notices are mailed to individuals on the mailing list(s) at least three weeks prior to the auction. Cash, cashiers check, money orders or travelers checks in increments of $100 or less are acceptable. Personal or business checks will be accepted if accompanied by a bank letter which guarantees payment. All Letters of Credit must be approved prior to the sale. There is a $20 fee to be included on the mailing list. (Fiscal year July 1–June 30.)

Indiana

State Surplus Property Section
1401 Milburn Street
Indianapolis, IN 46202
(317) 232-0134

Indiana holds auctions as items accumulate, mostly through sealed bids which are opened monthly and sold to the highest bidder. You will be asked to fill out a form specifying what category of items you are interested in bidding on. This procedure is for surplus property. Vehicles are sold on the first Wednesday of each month at 9:00 a.m. by public auction. Payment is by cash, certified check, cashiers check or money order. If you are interested in receiving their current mailing, send a self-addressed, stamped envelope to the above address requesting information.

Iowa

Department of Natural Resources
Wallace State Office Building
Des Moines, IA 50319
(515) 281-5145

The Department of Natural Resources holds an auction when a sufficient number of items have been gathered to warrant a sale. They don't hold one each year. Previous auctions have seen boats, fishing rods, tackle boxes, guns and other fishing and hunting equipment sold at bargain prices. Payment is by cash or check with appropriate identification. There is no mailing list, but auctions are advertised in local papers.

Department Of Transportation
(515) 239-1576

The DOT holds auctions seven times per year at 9:00 a.m. on Saturdays. They sell mostly patrol cars, pick-ups and trucks. Many have at least 80–90,000 miles of travel on them, and prices vary widely. A deposit of $200 is required on the day of the sale, with full payment due by the following Friday. Payment may be made by check or cash. Viewing is possible all day Friday and also Saturday morning prior to the sale.

Kansas

Kansas State Surplus Property
P.O. Box 19226
Topeka, KS 66619-0226
(913) 296-2334

The State Surplus Property office sells everything from sedans to bulldozers, and from staples to snow plows. Other merchandise may include confiscated cars from drug raids, office typewriters, and, very occasionally, even a buffalo! Property is first offered to other state agencies at set prices, and whatever is left over is opened to public sale at the same prices. A monthly catalog is published.

Kentucky

Kentucky Office of Surplus Property
514 Barrett Avenue
Frankfort, KY 40601
(502) 564-4836

Kentucky holds public auctions on Saturdays every two or three months. Items may include vehicles, desks, chairs, calculators, typewriters, file cabinets, tape recorders, electronic equipment, couches, beds, lawnmowers—and much, much more. Merchandise may be viewed the day before an auction. The office maintains a mailing list and also advertises upcoming auctions in local newspapers. Some items are auctioned by sealed bids. Acceptable payment methods are cash, check, or money order.

Louisiana

Division of Administration
Louisiana Property Assistance Agency
1059 Brickyard Lane
Baton Rouge, LA 70802
(504) 342-6849

Public auctions are held on the second Saturday of every month at 9:00 a.m. at 1502 North 17th Street. Items may be viewed the week before. Property sold ranges from medical and office equipment to boats, shop equipment, typewriters, file cabinets, pinball machines, bicycles, televisions, adding machines, chairs and vehicles. All items are sold "as is" and "where is". Payment is required in full the day of the auctions, but no personal or company checks are accepted. In addition, all merchandise must be removed within five days after the sale. Auctions are conducted by Braestone Auction Inc., 1680 O'Neal Lane #324, Baton Rouge, LA 70816.

Maine

Office of Surplus Property
Station 95
Augusta, ME 04333
(207) 287-5750

Five or six times per year, Maine publicly auctions off vehicles on the grounds of the Augusta Mental Health Institute. You must register to be able to bid before the start of the auction. Vehicles may include police cruisers, pick-up trucks, snowmobiles, lawnmowers and heavy equipment. Inspection is allowed between 8:00 a.m. and 10:00 a.m. the day of the auctions, which are generally held on Saturdays. Vehicles may be started up but not driven. Personal checks, money orders, certified checks and cash are all accepted. Office equipment and other non-vehicle items are sold by tag sale once each month, and prices are negotiable. Exact date, place and time of auctions are announced in local newspapers, but there is no mailing list.

Maryland

Maryland does not sell surplus property directly to the public. Office furniture and equipment are sold or donated to non-profit organizations or state agencies. Vehicles become state property after 60 days. If you would like more information, call: (410) 799-0440. State Property, P.O. Box 1039, 807 Brachs Bridge Road, Baltimore, MD 20794

Massachusetts

Massachusetts State Purchasing Agency
One Ashburton Place
Boston, MA 02108
FAX (617) 727-2920 or a recording (617) 727-7500

About six times each year, Massachusetts holds public auctions of surplus property. The State Purchasing Agency places ads in The Boston Globe on the Sunday prior to each of the auctions. Auctions usually take place on Saturday. Vehicles sold include sedans, wagons, vans and pick-ups which average four years of age. The condition of the property can vary greatly. Viewing is available the day before the auction from 9:00 a.m. to 4:00 p.m. No start-up allowed. The state does not currently auction other surplus property.

Michigan

State of Michigan, Department of Management and Budget
State Surplus Property
3353 Martin Luther King Blvd.
Lansing, MI 48913
(517) 335-8444

The state auctions off all kinds of office furniture, household goods, machinery, livestock and vehicles (including sedans, buses, trucks and boats). Auctions are held at different locations for the different categories of property. The State Surplus Property Office sends out yearly calendars with auction dates and information. Double check dates, because additions and changes can occur. Payment may be made by cash or check and should include the 6% state sales tax. No refunds are made. Inspections of merchandise are available either the day before or the morning of an auction.

Minnesota

Minnesota Surplus Operations Office
5420 Highway 8
New Brighton, MN 55112
(612) 639-4024, toll-free Hotline: 800-296-1056 (in-state only)

Minnesota holds about 13 auctions per year at various locations throughout the state. They sell vehicles such as patrol cars, passenger cars, trucks, vans, Suburbans; as well as tractors, boats, snowmobiles and outboard motors. The state also auctions off furniture, office equipment, kitchen equipment, tools and confiscated items, which include vehicles, computers, jewelry, car stereos and radios, as well as other personal property. Many of these items are sold FAR under market price. You can be put on the mailing list to receive a calendar for the schedule of upcoming auctions for the year. Inspections of property are held at 9:30 a.m., an hour and a half before the auction starts. Payment is by personal check, cash or money order.

Mississippi

Office of Surplus Property

P.O. Box 5778
Whitfield Road
Jackson, MS 39288
(601) 939-2050

Once a year Mississippi auctions off such items as machinery, textiles, ammunition boxes and vehicles. Merchandise can be viewed the day before, and is payable by cash or check with proper I.D.

Department of Public Safety

P.O. Box 958
Jackson, MS 39205
(601) 987-1453

Once or twice a year the State Department of Public Safety auctions off working vehicles. They have mostly Ford and Chevy patrol cars and occasionally vans and other types of vehicles. Most have at least 100,000 miles on them. Recent average prices ranged from $900 to $1500. Payment must be in cash or cashiers check — no personal checks. The balance is due the day of the auction. MidSouth Auctions can provide you with further information at (601) 956-2700.

Missouri

State of Missouri

Surplus Property Office
117 N. Riverside Drive
Jefferson City, MO 65102
(314) 751-3415

Missouri holds regular public auctions about twice a year, as well as holding sealed bid auctions every other month for merchandise located at various places across the state. Items sold include office equipment and vehicles. You can be put on a mailing list to receive notices of upcoming auctions, plus they are advertised in the local papers. For regular auctions, inspection is available the day of the auction. Sealed bid items may be viewed two or three days before the deadline. Items may be sold by lot or individually. Payment is in cash.

Montana

Property and Supply Bureau
930 Lyndale Avenue
Helena, MT 59620
(406) 444-4514

Montana holds a vehicle auction once a year. There are usually about 300 state vehicles. These auctions are advertised in local newspapers prior to the auction. In addition, the state offers other property for sale on the second Friday of each month. The sales include items such as office supplies, computers, chairs, tables, and vehicles including trucks, vans, sedans, highway patrol cars and much more. Payment can be by cash, business check or bank check.

Nebraska

Nebraska Office of Administrative Services
Material Division, Surplus Property
P.O. Box 94901
Lincoln, NE 68509
(402) 479-4890

Three or four times each year Nebraska auctions off office furniture, computers, and other surplus items. Separate auctions are held for vehicles and heavy equipment. Auctions are advertised in newspapers and on the radio. A mailing list is also maintained. Sealed bid auctions are held for property such as scrap iron, wrecked vehicles, guard posts and tires. Items are available for viewing two days prior to the auctions, which are held on Saturdays at 5001 S. 14th Street. Payment can be made by cash or check.

Nevada

Nevada State Purchasing Division
209 E. Muser
Room 304, Capitol Complex
Carson City, NV 89710
(702) 687-4070

About once a year Nevada holds a sale, usually on the second Saturday in August, of such items as calculators, desks, cabinets, tables, chairs, scrap metal, weapons, waste oil, and laboratory equipment. The sale is on a first come, first served basis, with minimum prices marked on the property. Occasionally prices of unsold items are reduced up to 50%. Vehicles, including motorcycles, as well as slot machines, are sold by auction generally two weeks after the first auction.

New Hampshire

Office of Surplus Property
78 Regional Drive, Bldg. 3
Concord, NH 03331
(603) 271-2126

New Hampshire holds two auctions per year of vehicles and other equipment, such as office furniture and machines. Vehicles, which include Omnis, cruisers, pick-ups and vans, may be viewed the day before the auction. Other merchandise can be viewed on the day of the auction. A mailing list is maintained and ads are also placed in local newspapers prior to the auctions. Acceptable forms of payment include cash and certified funds.

New Jersey

New Jersey Purchase and Property Distribution Center
1620 Stuyvesant Avenue
Trenton, NJ 08628
(609) 530-3300

New Jersey auctions off used state vehicles such as Chevy Chevettes, Dodge vans, various types of compact cars and occasionally buses and heavy equipment. Frequency of auctions is based on need. They can occur as often as every other week. Vehicles may be inspected and started up the day before the auction from 9:00 a.m. to 12:00 p.m. and from 1:00 p.m. to 3:00 p.m. Payment is by cash, money order, or certified check. No personal checks. A 10% deposit is required to hold a vehicle, and then the successful bidder has five days to complete payment and remove the vehicle. You can have your name added to their mailing list to be advised of upcoming auctions.

New Mexico

New Mexico Highway and Transportation Department, SB-2
P.O. Box 1149
Santa Fe, NM 87502-1149
(505) 827-5542 / 827-5587

Just about every year on a Saturday at the end of September, New Mexico auctions off vehicles. These include sedans, loaders, backhoes, snow removal equipment, pick-ups, vans, four-wheel drives and tractors. They also sell office equipment. You can place your name on their mailing list so you will be notified of the exact date of the auction together with descriptions of merchandise up for bidding. Items can be inspected the day before the auction. Payment is by cash, checks with proper I.D., money orders, or cashier's checks. No credit cards.

New York

State of New York, Office of General Service
Bureau of Surplus Property
Building #18, State Office Building Campus
Albany, NY 12226
(518) 457-6335

The Office of General Services holds auctions continuously in locations around the state. This includes surplus and used office equipment, scrap material, and agricultural items. Medical, photographic, institutional and maintenance equipment are sold through sealed bids, usually in lots of varying size. To participate in a sealed bid you place your name on a mailing list for items in several different categories, then make your bid by mail. The highest bidder wins and is notified by mail. Mailings give as much information as possible about the items being auctioned, but state officials stress that merchandise is sold "as is" and advise viewing the property in person prior to making a bid. A 10% deposit is required with each sealed bid. Vehicles are sold by public auction and may include cars, trucks, buses, and maintenance and construction equipment. Large items are sold individually, and smaller pieces of equipment, such as chain saws, are more likely to be sold in lots. Payment may be made by certified check or cash. A 10% deposit will hold a vehicle until the end of the day.

North Carolina

State Surplus Property
P.O. Box 33900
Raleigh, NC 27636-3900
(919) 733-3889

North Carolina auctions off surplus merchandise located throughout the state, including vehicles and office equipment, by sealed bid. Office equipment includes furniture, typewriters, desks, and chairs. Vehicles include Reliances, Crown Victorias, Mustangs and vans. For a fee of $15 ($25 for out-of-state) you can be placed on a mailing list to receive weekly advisories of what is for auction, with a description of the items and their condition. If you visit the warehouse in person you can pick up free samples of bid listings and look at lists of prices that items sold for at previous auctions. The warehouse is located on Highway 54 W. Old Chapel Hill Road. Payment is by money order or certified check, and you have 15 days to pay for your merchandise and pick it up. Items may be inspected two weeks before the auction from Monday to Friday between 8:00 a.m. and 4:45 p.m. On Tuesdays the warehouse is closed between 1:00 p.m. and 3:00 p.m. when the bids are opened. The public is then invited to attend.

North Dakota

Surplus Property Office
P.O. Box 7293
Bismarck, ND 58507
(701) 328-9665

Once a year the Office of Surplus Property auctions surplus office furniture and equipment, as well as vehicles and scrap materials. Merchandise may be viewed the morning of the auction. Cash, cashiers checks or money orders are acceptable forms of payment. Personal or business checks are accepted only with a bank letter of credit.

Ohio

Office of State and Federal Surplus Property
4200 Surface Road
Columbus, OH 43215
(614) 466-5052

Ohio holds public auctions and sealed bid sales on a wide range of office machines, equipment, furniture and vehicles. The sealed bid sales are held at various locations around the state for inoperable vehicles. These may be inspected any time after you receive your bid invitation in the mail. Other vehicle auctions are held three times a year, with inspections held the day before. At past auctions vehicles have included sedans, trucks, vans, 4x4's, boats, mowers, and tractors. At the time of the auction, a 25% down payment is required with the balance due by the following Monday. For the sealed bid auctions, payment must be made by money order or certified check.

Oklahoma

Central Purchasing
State Capitol
Oklahoma City, OK 73105
(405) 521-2129 : General information only for public auctions
(405) 521-3835: For information on sealed bids
(405) 521-2126: To get your name on a mailing list

Oklahoma auctions off vehicles as they accumulate. The state advertises upcoming auctions in local newspapers. Vehicles often have from 80,000 to 100,000 miles on them and vary greatly in condition. The agencies most likely to have auctions are: Department of Human Services (vehicles and other items); Wildlife Department (vehicles); Department of Public Safety (vehicles); and the Department of Transportation (vehicles). The state advises that you contact each agency separately for details. Sealed bid auctions of all kinds of merchandise are also held. You may request your name be placed on a mailing list, but if you don't bid for three consecutive times it will be removed. A catalog of listings is kept at the main office.

Oregon

Department of Surplus Property
1655 Salem Industrial Dr., NE
Salem, OR 97310
(503) 378-4714

About three times a year Oregon auctions off both vehicles and other equipment. Merchandise sometimes includes snow plows, horse trailers, computer equipment and ship equipment. To be placed on a mailing list you need to send a self-addressed, stamped envelope to the address listed above. Ads are also placed in local newspapers in the areas where auctions will be held. You may pay for merchandise with a 10% down payment, the balance due within three working days. Personal checks are accepted, but no title of ownership is sent until the check clears.

Pennsylvania

General Services Department
Bureau of Vehicle Management
2221 Forster Street
Harrisburg, PA 17105
(717) 783-3132

Vehicle auctions are held once a month. An inspection period starts two weeks prior to an auction, on Monday through Friday from 8:00 a.m. to 5:00 p.m. at the storage facility located at 22nd and Forster Streets in Harrisburg. If you request an application, you can have your name put on a mailing list for advance information on auctions for one year. A $100 deposit is required if you win a bid, with full payment due within five working days by cashier's check, certified check, or postal money order. No personal or company checks are accepted.

Bureau of Supplies and Surplus
Department of General Services
2221 Forster Street
Harrisburg, PA 17105
(717) 787-4083

The Bureau of Supplies and Surplus of the GSD sells such items as office furniture and machines, which include: typewriters, desks, chairs, sectional furniture, filing cabinets, copy machines, Dictaphones and calculators.

They also sell heavy construction equipment, dumptrucks, graders, etc. This merchandise is first offered to other state agencies, then put up for public sale after five days. There is no mailing list for notification of upcoming auctions, but ads are placed in the local newspapers in the area where the auction will be held. Property is sold at set prices. You may call to find out what items are currently for sale, or visit the warehouse between 8:00 a.m. and 3:45 p.m. Monday through Friday. The auctions are three times a year (Spring, Summer and Fall).

Rhode Island

Department of Administration
Division of Purchase
1 Capitol Hill
Providence, RI 02908
(401) 277-2375

Rhode Island's Division of Purchase auctions off its surplus vehicles and office equipment, as well as a variety of other items. Merchandise available varies greatly from auction to auction. Categories of merchandise include: automobile and transportation, food and food products; builders supplies, medical equipment, electronics and data processing items, furniture and furnishings, office machines and office supplies. Auctions for homes are held separately.

South Carolina

Division of General Services
1411 Boston Avenue
West Columbia, SC 29169
(803) 739-5490

South Carolina sells items ranging from vehicles and heavy equipment to office furniture. Property is collected in monthly cycles and offered first to state agencies before being put up for sale to the public. No mailing list is kept, but you can visit the warehouse between 8:00 a.m. and 4:30 p.m. Monday through Friday at 1441 Boston Avenue in West Columbia. Prices are tagged, so this is not really an auction. However, every other month the GSD holds public auctions of items by lot for State, Federal and Wildlife

Department property. A mailing list is kept for advance advisories and property descriptions. There is a $10 fee to receive the mailings. Items can be inspected, and you are advised to make notes of the numbers on property you are interested in so that you can check back to see if it's still available for sale, since State agencies have first choice.

South Dakota

Bureau of Administration
State Property Management
701 East Sioux Avenue
Pierre, SD 57501
(605) 773-4935

Twice a year, in the spring and the fall, the Department of Transportation holds public auctions for office equipment and vehicles. Vehicles have over 100,000 miles on them and sell for well under market price. You may visually inspect the vehicles prior to the auction, but you may not enter or start them up. The vehicles are started up and demonstrated during the auction. Auctions are located wherever the most property has accumulated in the state. Terms are cash only on the day of the sale.

Tennessee

Department of General Services Property Utilization
6500 Centennial Blvd.
Nashville, TN 37209
(615) 741-1711

Tennessee auctions off surplus vehicles, office equipment, and machinery of various kinds. The vehicles are of all types, including dump trucks, pickups, sedans and station wagons. Auctions are held between 8 and 9 times a year in Jackson, Dandridge, Nashville and Chattanooga. No mailing list is maintained, but the auctions are advertised in local newspapers. Payment can be in cash, cashier's checks or certified check.

Texas

Texas State Purchasing and General Services Commission
1711 San Jacinto
P.O. Box 13047, Capitol Station
Austin, TX 78711-3047
(512) 463-3445

Every two months Texas auctions off vehicles, office furniture and machines. You must apply to be put on the mailing list, which will give you a brief description of items available at the next auction. You can call the agency selling the property to arrange an inspection. Additionally, merchandise is available for inspection two hours prior to an auction. The auctions are held at the Austin City Coliseum. Items are mostly used state property, although some is confiscated merchandise as well. You must register to bid. Payment on a winning bid is due at the end of the auction. Cash, cashier's checks, certified check, money order, bank draft with Letter of Credit, or personal & company checks with Letters of Credit are acceptable forms of payment. Items sold on site must be removed the day of the sale. Texas also holds sealed bid auctions. Additionally, each of the Texas state agencies hold their own local sales. You must contact the individual agency to inquire about mailing lists.

Utah

Utah State Surplus Office
522 South 700 West
Salt Lake City, UT 84014
(801) 533-5885

Four or five times a year, Utah auctions off vehicles and other property. Most items are sold by public auction, although sealed bid auctions are sometimes held as well. Most of the public auctions are held in Salt Lake City at the above listed address, although some are occasionally held in other parts of the state. You may request your name be put on a mailing list to receive their auction fliers. Property may be viewed prior to an auction. Acceptable forms of payment are cash, cashier's check and personal checks up to $100 with two forms of I.D. Payment in full must be made the day of the auction.

Vermont

Vermont Central Surplus Property Agency
RD #2, Box 520
Montpelier, VT 05602
(802) 828-3394

Vermont sells low priced surplus office furniture and machines on a retail basis between 8:00 a.m. and 4:00 p.m. daily on Barre Montpelier Road. Items include desks, chairs, file cabinets and book shelves. Twice a year vehicles are sold by public auction, once in May and once in September. A mailing list is maintained to keep you informed of upcoming auctions. Local newspapers also advertise them. Vehicles can be inspected the Friday before an auction. Payment is up to the auctioneer. Generally, however, checks must be bank certified and a deposit is required to hold any vehicle not paid for in full the day of the auction. The balance is due by the following Tuesday at 3:00 p.m.

Virginia

State Surplus Property
P.O. Box 1199
Richmond, VA 23209
(804) 236-3666

Virginia auctions off everything but jewelry and land. Items include vehicles, tractors, bulldozers, dump trucks, pick-ups and vans, office equipment, computers, and office furniture. Scrap metal, tires and batteries are sold separately. Sales are by both public and sealed bid. There are sealed bid offerings every week, and as many as two auctions per week. Auction sites are at various locations around the state. You can get on a mailing list for both types of auctions. Inspections are allowed the day before the auction and again for a couple of hours on the day of the auction.

Washington

Office of Commodity Redistribution
2805 'C' Street, SW
Building 5, Door 49
Auburn, WA 98001
(206) 931-3931

Washington holds auctions of used state vehicles, conducts silent bid auctions, and also sells surplus materials by sealed bids. The vehicles are auctioned about every three months, and include all kinds of used state automobiles. There are a few new luxury or confiscated type vehicles. The silent bids are held once a month, and include large quantities of office furniture sold by the pallet, with the exception of typewriters, which are sold on an individual basis. You may visit the warehouse to inspect the items before the auction. Payment may be in the form of cashier's check, money order, or cash. No personal checks are accepted. For the sealed bids, you can call for a catalog of merchandise which includes everything from vehicles to scrap material, office equipment, computers, clothes, cleaning fluids, tools and pumps. If you wish to get on their mailing list, contact the number listed above.

West Virginia

West Virginia State Agency Surplus Property
2700 Charles Avenue
Dunbar, WV 25064
(304) 348-3456

Each month West Virginia auctions off all kinds of office equipment, furniture and vehicles. The vehicles range from police cruisers to the occasional Mercedes—all in various conditions. Inspection is available the week before the auction from 8:30 a.m. to 6:00 p.m. Payment may be by personal check, business check or certified check. No cash. Payment is due in full the day of the auction. For sealed bids, payment is due within one week after a bid has won. Deposits (usually 20% of the bid) are returned to unsuccessful bidders.

Wisconsin

Department of Transportation
Hill Farm Building
4802 Sheboygan Avenue
Madison, WI 53707
(608) 266-3620

The Department of Transportation continuously sells a variety of items from its warehouse in Madison. Items vary greatly from week to week. Items are sold at set prices and can be viewed at the warehouse, but you need to call ahead to make an appointment.

Wisconsin Department of Administration
P.O. Box 7880
Madison, WI 53708
(608) 266-8024

The Department of Administration holds vehicle auctions every month— usually with about 100 vehicles available at any given time. They also hold computer auctions about every six months. All different makes and models of vehicles are sold, and they usually are at least four years old and have 70,000+ miles on them. You can get your name put on their mailing list for advance notice of auctions, but they are also advertised in the newspaper. Payment is by cash, personal check, cashier's check or money order. No credit cards. The full amount is due the day of the sale.

Wyoming

State Motor Pool
723 West 19th Street
Cheyenne, WY 82002
(307) 777-7247

Although it donates most of its surplus property to other state agencies, Wyoming does auction off its surplus vehicles. These include pick-ups, vans, sedans and jeeps. Most have high mileage, but not always. You can get your name put on their mailing list to receive advance notice of upcoming auctions. They are also advertised in local newspapers. Inspection of the vehicles is available between 3:00 p.m. and 5:30 p.m. the Friday before the auction. Payment depends on the auctioneer conducting the auction.

Department of the T   sury / Internal Revenue Service

Notice of

Public Auction Sale

Under the authority in Internal Revenue Code section 6331, the property described below has been seized for nonpayment of internal revenue taxes due from

_____

The property will be sold at public auction as provided by Internal Revenue Code section 6335 and related regulations.

Date of Sale: _____December 21,_____ 19_____

Time of Sale: _____10:00_____ am ~~pm~~

Place of Sale: Internal Revenue Service Lobby

Title Offered: Only the right, title, and interest of _____
in and to the property will be offered for sale. If requested, the Internal Revenue Service will furnish information about possible encumbrances, which may be useful in determining the value of the interest being sold (See the back of this form for further details.)

Description of Property: Assessors Parcel Number 079-060-50
Real Property in the unincorporated area of the County of Santa Barbara, State of California, described as:

Government Lot 2 and the West half of the Southeast quarter of the northwest quarter of Section 30, Township 5 North, Range 29 West, San Bernardino Base and Meridian in the County of Santa Barbara, State of California, containing approximately 28.15 acres more or less.

The East ½ of the Southeast ¼ of the Northwest ¼ of Section 30, Township 5 North, Range 29 West, San Bernardino Base and Meridian, in the County of Santa Barbara, State of California.

TOGETHER WITH an undivided 20/96ths water rights as set out in Agreement dated April 12, 1971, recorded April 15, 1971 as Instrument number 10739, Book 2343, Page 1281 in the office of the county recorder of said county.

Government Lot 1 of Section 30, Township 5 North, Range 29 West, San Bernardino Base and Meridian, in the County of Santa Barbara, State of California.

TOGETHER WITH an undivided 8/96ths water rights as set out in Agreement dated April 12, 1971, recorded April 15, 1971 as Instrument number 10739, Book 2343, Page 1281 in the office of the county recorder of said county.

Property may be Inspected at: By appointment. Contact _____ Revenue Officer for appointment.

Payment Terms:
☐ Full payment required on acceptance of highest bid
☒ Deferred payment as follows: 20% of purchase price upon acceptance of highest bid with balance to be paid no later than one week after the sale.

Form of Payment: All payments must be by cash, certified check, cashier's or treasurer's check or by a United States postal, bank, express, or telegraph money order. Make check or money order payable to the Internal Revenue Service.

| Signature *W Skallenberger* | Name and Title *(Typed)*   Revenue Officer | Date 11-18- |
| Address for information About the Sale   Internal Revenue Service | | Phone |

Form **2434** (Rev. 3-84)

Chapter 11:
The Internal Revenue
Service

> "I just bought a 150 year old hotel at auction last month. Talk about a steal! I had the winning bid of $18,600—unbelievable! The place is an historic landmark, which means I will be able to get government money to assist with the renovation. I've already got 4 businesses leasing space from me, which covers all of my expenses. Now any new leases I negotiate are pure profit for me."
>
> G. Weller

Internal Revenue Service (IRS) auctions are well worth attending. You stand an excellent chance of finding a really good deal. You never know what you'll find either, so it's really fun. They sell literally everything under the sun. If you take a look around your home and/or your neighbor's property, the businesses downtown — any of these could be on the IRS auction block.

When individuals or corporations don't pay on time, don't pay enough, disagree with IRS policies or make a fuss about IRS collection tactics, they become prime candidates for having their personal property and real estate seized.

The IRS is part of the Executive Branch of our government under the Department of the U.S. Treasury. It's interesting to note that the U.S. Tax Court, which is where official authorization comes to seize property, is under the jurisdiction of the Legislative Branch of Congress. Amazingly, most IRS auctions are held with only local and internal authorization. The

IRS seems to make up its own rules as it goes along. They give themselves authority by writing their own manuals and codes. Seizure comes about from Internal Revenue Code section 6331.

IRS auctions are definitely ones you should try to attend. When a $12,000 car is sold for $1,200 and the IRS is still owed $10,800, the poor taxpayer gets billed the difference. So the IRS doesn't really seem to care how much items sell for, since they are going to collect their money regardless. This is where you, with your inside knowledge, are going to cash in handsomely!

The only area which can prove less than satisfactory when it comes to buying at an IRS auction is the 180 day period which is given to taxpayers in which they can redeem their property. In other words, if you buy a car, house, television, computer, etc. at an IRS auction and the taxpayer is able to come up with the money to pay their back taxes, you will have to forfeit your purchase. This can be particularly sticky when it comes to real estate. It doesn't happen very often, since it's usually quite difficult for someone to not only come up with the money they owe—but the interest and penalties as well. Especially when these can often double or triple the original amount owed!

Like the U.S. Marshals Service auctions, the IRS auctions are decentralized. What this means to you is that you are going to have to be tenacious when it comes to getting the information you are seeking, but once again, this will put you way ahead of your competition, since most of them won't take the time.

IRS Public Auctions

At the end of this chapter we have provided you with telephone numbers for IRS auction information. The Hotline phone numbers should be recorded messages which give you information about upcoming sales. Not all areas have Hotline numbers available. Some areas will send you a bidders list, which tells of upcoming sales in your area. Other areas simply advertise in the local Sunday newspapers. The IRS also places auction notices in local post offices.

If we don't list a telephone number for an IRS office in your area, call your local IRS office and ask if they have a Hotline phone number for IRS seized property sales in your area. If they don't, ask if they send out bidders lists for seized property sales. If you call an IRS office and the operator tells you they don't know anything about any auctions, ask to speak to the Collection Division. When you've reached this department, ask them to send you any notices of public or sealed bid auctions. The announcements are made on Form 2434 — so you may have to refresh their memory by asking specifically for that particular form. On page 90 is a copy of an IRS auction notice on their Form 2434 so you can familiarize yourself with what they look like.

When calling the IRS, you may be given the following toll-free number to call: 1-800-829-1040. We DO NOT recommend calling this number. This is basically a number to call to order tax forms or ask tax-related questions, and they usually are not able to provide you with regional telephone numbers for seized property sales.

E. G. & G. Dynatrend also handles some IRS auctions. While they do primarily handle sales of seized property for the U.S. Customs Service (see Chapter 12), they have begun to sell property seized by the Criminal Investigation Division of the IRS. You can call the E. G. & G. Public Auction Line (PAL) at (703) 351-7887. If you prefer to write, their address is:

E. G. & G. Dynatrend
2300 Clarendon Blvd., Suite 705
Arlington, VA 22201
(703) 273-7373

IRS auctions are, fortunately for you, not particularly well planned or advertised unless someone famous is going on the auction block. So don't hold your breath for an auction calendar or a schedule of any kind. The auctions are held sporadically as tax seized items accumulate.

As soon as you receive an auction notice, you'll see that it doesn't look like any other invitation for bids you may have received. Nor does it resemble the flyers auctioneers send out. At first glance you may even think your property is being auctioned. Take a deep breath and read on.

Details are explained on the form. There is a contact phone number and name at the bottom of the form which you can call if you have any questions. The majority of what you need to know is on the form, including a brief description of the items. You will want to confirm the accuracy of what's included and also ask about the condition of anything you are considering buying. Make sure the auction is still being held.

IRS Sealed Bid Sales

Sealed bid sales are a staple of the IRS auction system. Even at their public auctions, bidders are many times given the opportunity of mailing in a bid rather than attending in person. The only way a sealed bid is accepted by the IRS is by using Form 2222. You can obtain one from the IRS branch holding the sale.

There are some areas in the country which have IRS hotline numbers. When you call you will be able to listen to a tape recorded description of upcoming auctions. You will be given additional information on how to contact someone if you are interested in more data.

You can take advantage of the fact that so many people are squeamish about attending IRS auctions. There are some really great deals to be had! It's not unheard of for someone to walk away with an entire business valued at $50,000 or more for only a couple of thousand dollars.

All the IRS is trying to get is owed back taxes. While they may claim to demand a minimum bid or have a reserve policy, the real deal is somewhat different. More often than not, they will sell to the highest bidder regardless of the minimum bid or reserve price. They are in the business of collecting taxes, not of holding auctions.

Full payment is required immediately upon acceptance of your winning bid. Since they auction off real estate, you can work out terms — sometimes 30 to 45 days — but you'll have to put a down payment of about 20%. The method of payment is cash, certified check, cashier's check or money order, made out to you know who — the IRS.

On the following pages we have provided you with several Hotline numbers that the IRS currently offers, as well as numbers to contact to request bidders lists. If you are interested in attending an IRS auction, contact them by telephone to obtain information about upcoming auctions. Be sure to let us know if you find a Hotline phone number that we don't have listed. We will include it in our next printing and send you an updated Volume 2 auction listing with our thanks.

Internal Revenue Service Hotline Phone Numbers

Anchorage, AK	(907) 271-6392	Indianapolis, IN	(317) 226-5946
Laguna Niguel, CA	(714) 643-4523	St. Paul, MN	(612) 290-4042
Los Angeles, CA	(213) 894-5777	Brooklyn, NY	(718) 488-2717
Sacramento, CA	(916) 974-5923	Las Vegas, NV	(702) 455-1034
San Francisco, CA	(510) 839-1040	Cincinatti, OH	(513) 684-2514
San Jose, CA	(408) 494-8500	Cleveland, OH	(216) 522-7902
Central, FL	(407) 660-5868	Portland, OR	(503) 326-7840
South, FL	(941) 688-8439	Philadelphia, PA	(412) 355-2534
North, FL	(904) 279-1656	Dallas, TX	(214) 767-1386
Atlanta, GA	(800) 829-9348		(Bidders list)
Honolulu, HI	(808) 541-1104	Seattle, WA	(206) 220-5461
Boise, ID	(208) 334-1360	Milwaukee, WI	(414) 297-1292

Insider Tip

IRS auctions are really bankruptcy sales. Because there is no set policy for their sales there are GREAT deals for those of you "in the know"! At IRS auctions, the bidders always come out winners. These auctions are well worth finding out about and attending.

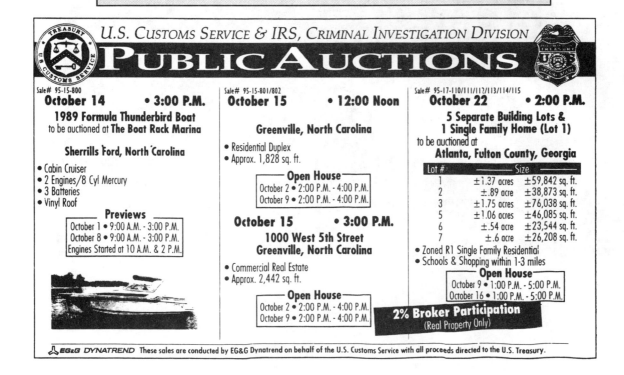

Chapter 12:
U. S. Customs Auctions

"I recently attended an auction with a friend. We were amazed at the quality and quantity of merchandise offered there. They were auctioning off loads of antiques, silver, paintings, collectibles, and jewelry. In addition there were many newer items, such as video and electronic equipment, computers, and even horse tack! Talk about having something for everyone! Since this was our first auction we just watched. Next time we're going to bid!"

C. Baylies

These auctions include all types of cars, aircraft, vessels such as yachts and sailboats, real estate, computer equipment and electronics, and personal property such as jewelry, clothing and household items. The type, quality and condition of the goods vary widely. The sales take place nationwide. High value aircraft and vessels are advertised in newspapers and trade publications.

The U.S. Customs Service does not hold its own auctions. They currently utilize the services of **E. G. & G. Dynatrend,** which is a private auction company. Customs auctions are held regularly at ten different auction sites across the country on a rotating basis. More locations may be added in the future, but they currently are handled as follows:

Eastern United States:
Edison, New Jersey
Miami/Ft. Lauderdale, Florida
San Juan, Puerto Rico

Central United States:
El Paso, Texas
Edinburg, Texas
Laredo, Texas

Western United States:
Los Angeles, California
Chula Vista, California
Nogales, Arizona
Yuma, Arizona

E. G. & G. Dynatrend maintains a public auction line, known as **PAL.** You can call it at (703) 273-7373 anytime to hear their tape recorded message. This gives information about upcoming Customs auctions being held across the U.S. Their message will give you the auction location, date and time of the auction, as well as a brief and general description of the items being auctioned.

The taped message will instruct you on how you need to proceed in order to obtain a sample auction flier. A sample can be sent to you free of charge.

If you want to receive regular auction notices, you can get an annual subscription, which runs $25 to $50 depending upon whether you wish a regional or national edition. The regional listings are broken down into two regions; the Eastern region, which covers auctions east of the Mississippi River and including Puerto Rico. The Western region covers information on auctions west of the Mississippi River including Alaska. The nationwide listing provides listings of U.S. Customs auctions in the continental United States, Alaska, and Puerto Rico. You may subscribe by calling the public auction line at (703) 273-7373 or by contacting them at:

E. G. & G. Dynatrend
U.S. Customs Service Support Division
2300 Clarendon Blvd., Suite 705
Attn: Subscriptions
Arlington, VA 22201

In addition to this subscription service, U.S. Customs auctions are also frequently advertised in the *Los Angeles Times, New York Times, Miami*

Herald, Wall Street Journal, and the *Newark Star Ledger.* You may also come across advertisements in local newspapers and various trade journals. Another source for Customs auctions notices is local U.S. Customs Service offices.

Before attending a Customs auction you will want to pick up a copy of the auction catalog. The catalogs are available free, and can be obtained from the auction site and from selected inspection locations before the auction. The catalog provides you with information on the specific items available for auction, the lot numbers, and terms of sale.

Check the inspection schedules and make time to preview the merchandise to be auctioned. The items to be auctioned are usually not available for inspection during the auction. Also these items are not always located at the actual auction site. The auction catalog will provide you with information on where the auction preview as well as the auction itself will be held.

Once you find the items or lots that you are interested in bidding on, make sure you register to bid. There is no charge to register, and you may do so at the auction site before the auction or also at some inspection locations. When you register you will be asked to fill out a bidder registration form and present a photo I.D. Upon completion of the form, you will be given a bidder number.

Customs merchandise is sold by the lot. At some of their public auctions you may be allowed to submit a sealed bid by registered mail with an accompanying cashier's check. When a sealed bid has been received on an item, the sealed bid will be the starting bid for that lot. If your bid is not successful, they will return your check by certified mail.

If you have made a successful bid, you need to pick up a notice of award (NOA) at the cashier. This is your paid receipt which allows you to pick up the items you've purchased. Full payment is expected at this time by cash or cashier's check. Some locations even accept credit cards. As a general rule, if your total purchases equal $5,000 or less, full payment on the day of the auction will be required. For total purchases over $5,000 a minimum deposit of $5,000 is required on the day of the auction and the balance will be due in full the following business day.

You will be required to remove your auction winnings by the date specified in the terms of sale. Otherwise you will be billed for storage. If you fail to pick up your merchandise it will be forfeited. If the merchandise you purchase is for export-only, it generally has to be shipped out of the states within 30 days.

For those of you interested in items which can be sold for export-only, you'll want to be sure you have foreign buyers or brokers lined up before you buy, so you don't have to run around at the last minute trying to resell the items you've successfully bid on. Items sold as "export only" cannot be registered used or resold in the United States. They must be exported from the U.S. within a specified time frame.

When you are attending a U.S. Customs Service auction, take a few cashier's checks in small denominations ($100s and $20s) which are made out to yourself, rather than one large check made out to E. G. & G. Dynatrend. If you don't buy anything, you can simply put them back in your account. E. G. & G. Dynatrend doesn't usually give change back on checks for more than 10% of the amount of the cashier's check.

It is not uncommon for agents or attorneys of drug dealers to go to these auctions with loads of money so that they can buy back their client's property. When this occurs, it can drive up the prices being paid. If you happen to attend an auction where this happens—stay out of the bidding. You're going to end up paying too high a price if you happen to be successful.

One added benefit of buying at U.S. Customs auctions is that the successful bidder is not responsible for any liens that may have been levied against a particular item. After you pay for an item it is transferred to you free and clear of any liens.

There are many great bargains to be found at the U.S. Customs Service auctions. Their auctions are professionally run, and it is easy to obtain information about upcoming auctions and what is being put on the block.

For further information about U.S. Customs Service auctions, give PAL a call at (703) 273-7373. Their system is highly sophisticated and will provide you with the information you need to locate the sales you wish to attend. While you are on the line, you will be given an opportunity to subscribe to their auction mailings. Remember that you can call the Public Access Line 24 hours a day. Their information is available in English and Spanish. You will first hear a recorded message and can press the number as shown below to correspond with the particular topic or area you wish information on:

Press 1: Subscription Information
Press 2: General Program Information
Press 3: Eastern States Auction Information
Press 4: Central States Auction Information
Press 5: Western States Auction Information
Press 6: Real Property Information
Press 7: Comments
Press 8: Miami Sales Information

Press 9: Edison Sales Information

Press 0: Customer Service Representative
(available Monday thru Friday, 8:00 a.m. - 5:00 p.m. EST)

United States Customs Service
in conjunction with
Secret Service
IRS - Criminal Investigation Division

AUCTION DATE & TIME:

AUCTION LOCATION:
Broward County/Greater Ft. Lauderdale
Convention Center

FEATURING:

- 1989 BMW 325i Convertible
- 1989 Chevrolet Corvette
- 1988 Jaguar XJS Convertible
- Baby Diapers, 480bls
- Diamonds, Loose
- Engelhard Silver Bars, 47ea
- Jewelry
- Mercury Outboard Engines, 2ea
- Rolex Watches, export only
- Shoes, OVER 8,000 PAIRS!
- Wearing Apparel, 367ctns
- & Much More!

1989 BMW 325i Convertible

EG&G DYNATREND This sale is conducted by EG&G Dynatrend on behalf of the U.S. Customs Service, the Internal Revenue Service (Criminal Investigation Division), and the Secret Service with all proceeds directed to the U.S. Treasury. Sale #95-52-001/002/702812. LLA #AB427

UNITED STATES GENERAL SERVICES ADMINISTRATION

Public Auction

November 30 & December 1
Cobb Galleria Centre
Atlanta, Georgia

OVER 1300 VARIOUS PERSONAL PROPERTY ITEMS RECEIVED BY GOVERNMENT AGENCIES UNDER PUBLIC LAW 103-123

Immediately following the sale of the U.S. Marshals seized assets, Manheim will be selling personal property received by the General Services Administration (GSA) from various federal agencies. This merchandise consists of several hundred different items, many suitable for gift giving. Among the lots to be sold are Rolex Watches, Mont Blanc and Waterman Pens, Gucci Scarves and Wallets, Minolta/Canon/Nikon Cameras and many other valuables including:

Albums	Clocks	Electronics	Mugs	Shawls
Ashtrays	Clothing	Fabric	Napkin Holders	Shirts
Baskets	Coasters	Fans	Neckties	Signs
Bedspreads	Coffee Sets	Figurines	Ornaments	Skis
Belts	Coffee Tables	Flatware	Paintings	Slippers
Binoculars	Coins	Goblets	Paper Weights	Statues
Blankets	Cosmetics	Hanging Lights	Pens	Suit
Blouses	Crystal	Hats	Perfume	Sun Glasses
Books	Cups and Saucers	Incense Burners	Photographs	Sweaters
Bowls	Daggers	Jewelry	Pillow Covers	Swords
Boxes	Desk Sets	Jewelry Boxes	Placemats	Tables
Briefcases	Dessert Sets	Knives	Plaques	Tablecloths
Cameras	Diaries	Lamps	Plates	Tea Sets
Candelabras	Directory	Lighters	Porcelain Egg	Trays
Cases	Discs (CDs)	Linens	Portfolios	Vases
Chairs	Dishes	Luggage	Purses	Video Tapes
Chess Sets	Dolls	Maps	Rugs	Wall Hangings
Chests	Door Hangings	Mirrors	Scarves	Wallets
Cigar Boxes	Dresses	Models	Sculptures	Watches

Chapter 13:
The General Services Administration (GSA)

> "When you attend a GSA vehicle auction the cars are sold by a certain criteria. Small cars (sedans like a Corsica) are sold at 3 years or 36,000 miles. Trucks (4-wheel drive, Dodge Rams and utility trucks) are sold at 5 years or 50,000 miles, and big trucks are sold at 6 years or 60,000 miles. I was told that if something major goes wrong with a vehicle purchased at auction from the GSA that they will negotiate to make things right for you."
>
> S. Stewart

This agency plays a crucial role when it comes to government merchandise auctions. Fortunately for you, auctions don't play a major role in the overall duties for which the GSA is responsible. This means you can find terrific bargains.

The GSA was created to manage government property and records. They are the agency supervising the construction and operation of government buildings. Additionally, they procure and distribute the supplies used by the federal government. They are also responsible for civilian traffic and communications facilities, which means they handle the computer facilities for the government in addition to stockpiling vital materials and equipment.

The GSA is involved in two diverse types of auctions; personal property/merchandise/equipment/vehicles AND real estate. Personal property auctions are handled through the Federal Service Supply Bureaus of the GSA. Real estate sales are held by the GSA's Federal Property Resource Service.

The items the GSA auctions come from several branches of government. These include: the Department of the Interior, the U.S. Fish and Wildlife Services, the Bureau of Land Management, the Federal Communications Commission, the Immigration and Naturalization Service, the U.S. Border Patrol, the U.S. Department of Labor, the FBI, the IRS and the Department of Energy, to name just a few. Merchandise sold by the GSA at auction for the various governmental agencies is strictly their surplus equipment. In addition to vehicles and surplus properties, the GSA oversees a program run by the Federal Property Resource Service (FPRS). This is a nationwide organization which sells property no longer needed by the federal government.

The GSA does not generally sell items which have been confiscated from criminals or tax offenders. We say "not generally" because the Marshals Service sometimes turns over automobiles and other properties for the GSA to auction on their behalf.

The GSA holds two types of auctions — public and sealed bid sales. The GSA is well known for its sales of surplus vehicles. In the past few years, the GSA has started handling the disposition of the U.S. Marshals Service's seized merchandise. Since the Marshals Service tends to bust high rollers, much of the merchandise they confiscate leans toward luxury. You can thank the Marshals Service for most of the flash you'll see at a GSA auction! This is where you'll most likely run into the fantastic bargains on fancy cars like Mercedes, BMW's, Jaguars, Ferraris, etc.

Exactly what sort of bargain can you expect? This depends a great deal on YOU. The old saying, "being at the right place at the right time" certainly holds true when it comes to auctions. There are many instances of people who have successfully bid $100 to $200 and come away with a used car in excellent condition. In fact, the auctioneers we have spoken to all say it is not unrealistic to expect a winning bid to be one half or less of the wholesale price! Meaning 10 cents to 20 cents on the retail dollar! That's right—50% below **wholesale.**

It doesn't take a rocket scientist to see that bargains abound! Remember when we said earlier that the GSA handles lots of auctions, but this isn't their main focus? Well, this is where your opportunity really presents itself with GSA auctions. While they do have highly professional people working with them at auctions, they deal with so much merchandise in such vast quantities that they cannot possibly keep track of the actual value of each and every item.

Since we've mentioned luxury cars, let's use that as an example. When a drug bust occurs and merchandise is confiscated, how do you think the items are valued? Certainly the federal agencies use some of the same tools you or I would to determine value. If they have confiscated a 1993 Corvette, Mercedes or BMW, you can bet they will take a quick look in the Blue Book or talk to a trusted dealer about the worth of said vehicle. HOWEVER, and this is a big HOWEVER, exactly what will the sale of this automobile (or when we're talking IRS or drug busts — boat, or home, or jewelry) be expected to recover for the government?

The government is trying to recoup monies they think are owed to them because the busted individual has made money and not shared what they should with Uncle Sam. What do they really owe? Your guess is as good as mine — or theirs! It's not uncommon to hear about drug busts where hundreds of thousands of dollars have been confiscated along with cars, furs, jewelry, etc. The actual money that has been seized goes to the government. When it comes to the cars, furs, jewelry — ANY money they are able to realize is a plus. Why should you get a bargain? BECAUSE IT'S YOUR TAX DOLLARS AT WORK, that's why!!!

This is why luxury items so often are auctioned for pennies on the dollar. While the Lincoln Continental, Mercedes, Jaguar or BMW auctioned by the GSA may hold the same value as a similar car obtained under different circumstances—ANY amount it brings at auction is money ahead for the government.

HOTLINES: The GSA relies quite heavily on hotline tape recordings to inform you about the date, time and location of upcoming auctions. Often times their recording will provide you with the phone numbers and locations for contacts on specific auctions. At the end of this chapter we have provided

you with a list of the different hotline regions and telephone numbers, along with additional information.

Anyone interested in attending is invited to show up at the auction site to participate. Due to the expense of mailing information, the GSA is not very aggressive about getting auction flyers to the public. It is up to you to demand auction catalogs, brochures or flyers.

Even when you call their hotline number and listen to the tape recorded messages, it is wise to also contact the regional office involved for an auction flyer. Since the information on the hotline is limited, be sure to write down the public sale number. This tells you which auction you are interested in. Then, when you call the regional office, you will be able to tell them exactly which flyer you want to receive.

Individuals interested in participating in sealed bid sales need to contact the regional office in their state and request an application form. You will be sent GSA Form 2170, which is called the Surplus Personal Property Mailing List Application. It needs to be completed as follows:

1. Write your name and full address in the space provided. We suggest you use a pen and PRINT neatly.

2. Mark the geographic area that interests you. You can select a couple, but don't put down more than four.

3. Unless you're a scrap dealer, you'll want to select "usable" as the category of goods you are interested in hearing about.

4. Be sure to put postage on the form and mail it in.

5. You should begin receiving fliers within two to six weeks. These are called Invitations For Bid (IFB) and will contain instructions on how to participate and whether or not deposits will be required with your bid.

The sealed bid sales offer some of the best bargains. There are some great bargains in the office equipment area. It is common for someone to bid less than a hundred dollars to purchase computer equipment worth several thousand!

Since all merchandise is owned by the government, the buyer gets clear title to it. You will have a deadline (30 days or less) for payment and removing purchased items from storage. Transportation and shipping arrangements are up to the new owner.

Once you've made the winning bid and paid for your purchase, make sure you get a receipt. At vehicle auctions you are given Standard Form 97. On other items you will need to ask for a Certificate of Release with the bill of sale. These provide you with title to the items purchased.

Payment by cash, cashier's check, money order or certified check is the norm. A few offices have started taking bank credit cards. Again, as we've told you before, read the conditions of sale in the auction catalog before bidding.

A rule of thumb for all government agency auctions—pay for your purchase. NEVER walk away at the end of the auction without paying if you've had the successful bid. When you buy the property you must pay for it. If you don't you may be banned from any future bidding at ALL federal government auctions.

Remember that your copy of Volume 2 of this directory also includes a state-by-state listing of some of the GSA auctions held nationwide. While we recommend you contact the GSA office in your area (using the addresses and phone numbers we have provided at the end of this chapter), you will also want to refer to your Volume 2 directory to see if we have listed an upcoming auction in your area.

Regional Contacts and Hotline Numbers

Federal Supply Service Bureau Directory
Office of Sales
General Information (800) GSA-1313

National Capitol Region

Serves: Metro DC, Montgomery & Prince George's Counties, MD; Fairfax, Arlington, Prince William Counties plus Alexandria and Falls Church, VA

National Surplus & Sales Center
Federal Supply Service Bureau
6808 Loisdale Road
Springfield, VA 22150
(703) 557-7785
Hotline: (703) 557-7796

Region One

Serves: Connecticut, Maine, Massachusetts, New Hampshire, Rhode Island, Vermont. Auctions held every other week, sealed bids held monthly.

Federal Supply Service Bureau
10 Causeway Street 4#2FBP-1
Boston, MA 02222
(617) 565-7322
Hotline: (617) 565-7326

Region Two

Serves: New Jersey, New York, Puerto Rico, Virgin Islands

Federal Supply Service Bureau
26 Federal Plaza #2FBB-2
New York, NY 10278
(212) 264-4824
Hotline: (212) 264-4824
Toll Free: (800) 488-SALE

Region Three

Serves: Delaware, Maryland, Pennsylvania, Virginia, West Virginia

Federal Supply Service Bureau
Personal Property Sales Section
841 Chestnut Street, Suite 540
Philadelphia, PA 19107
(215) 597-6574
Hotline: (215) 656-3400

Region Four

Serves: Alabama, Florida, Georgia, Kentucky, Mississippi, North Carolina, South Carolina, Tennessee

General Services Administration
404 West Beach Street #4FBB
Atlanta, GA 30365
(404) 331-3064
Hotline: (404) 331-5177
Fax: (404) 331-1877

Region Five

Serves: Illinois, Indiana, Michigan, Minnesota, Ohio, Wisconsin

General Services Administration
Federal Supply Service Bureau
Sales Services, Mail Staff 34-5
230 S. Dearborn Street
Chicago, IL 60604
(312) 353-5504 or 353-6064
Hotline: (312) 353-0246

Region Six

Serves: Iowa, Kansas, Missouri, Nebraska

Excess Property Sales
GSA Federal Supply Bureau #6FP-P
4400 College Blvd., Suite 175
Overland Park, KS 66211
(816) 823-3700
Hotline: (816) 823-3714

Region Seven

Serves: Arkansas, Louisiana, New Mexico, Oklahoma, Texas

General Services Administration
819 Taylor Street
Fort Worth, TX 76102
(817) 334-2352

Region Eight

Serves: Colorado, Montana, North Dakota, Utah, Wyoming

General Services Administration
Federal Supply Service Bureau
Building 41
Denver Federal Center
Denver, CO 80226
(303) 236-7698

Region Nine

Serves: Arizona, Northern California, Guam, Hawaii, Nevada

General Services Administration
450 Golden Gate Avenue
San Francisco, CA 94102 4th Floor
(415) 774-5240, San Francisco
(415) 522-2891, Personal Property
(415) 522-3429, Real Estate
(415) 522-3030, Fleet Management Center

Sacramento
(916) 366-2044

Southern California:

General Services Administration
5600 Rickenbacker Road
Building 5E
Bell, CA 90201
(213) 526-7496

Region Ten:

Serves: Idaho, Oregon, Washington

General Services Administration
Excess Personal Property Sales
400 15th Street SW
Auburn, WA 98001
(206) 931-7566
Hotline: (206) 931-7763
Vehicles, every 3rd Thursday: (206) 931-7950

On the following page we show you an actual listing of some of the vehicles that were offered at a recent General Services Administration (GSA) auction. Note the low mileage on many of the vehicles offered—most of these vehicles have less than 50,000 miles on them. **Several have less than 15,000 miles on them!** When was the last time you had a chance to get a GREAT DEAL on a car with less than 15,000 miles on the odometer?

public notice:

Seeking that well maintained, vehicle?
DETERMINE YOUR OWN PRICE!

AUCTION

SALE NUMBER: 91FBPS–94–089

001 **PICKUP:** 1988 CHEVROLET 2500, 4X4, 8 CYL, TAG:G63–13994, EST MI: 51,532, VIN:1GCFK24K7JZ228554. (479A654208 #1395)

002 **PICKUP:** 1988 CHEVROLET S10, 6 CYL, TAG:G40–03040, EST MI: 31,256, VIN:1GCCS14R0J8167211. (479A654208 #1396)

003 **SEDAN:** 1990 CHEVROLET CORSICA, 4 CYL, TAG:G12–73683, EST MI: 22,071, VIN:1G1LT54G7LY212157. (479A654208 #1397)

004 **UTILITY MAINT:** 1987 DODGE DAKOTA, 6 CYL,TAG:G41–76004, EST MI: 34,324, VIN:1B7GN14M4HS506725. (479A654208 #1398)

005 **PASS UTILITY:** 1987 DODGE CARAVAN, 7 PASS, 6 CYL, TAG:G40–03026, EST MI: 53,447, VIN:2B4FK2136HR295161. (479A654208 #1399)

006 **CARGO VAN:** 1987 DODGE B250, 6 CYL, TAG:G42–48349, EST MI: 51,506, VIN:2B7HB23H9HK312192. (479A654208 #1400)

007 **PICKUP:** 1990 DODGE DAKOTA, 4X4 STD. TRANS, 6 CYL, TAG:G61–20100, EST MI: 68,572,VIN:1B7GG26X2LS688196. (479A654208 #1401)

008 **SEDAN:** 1993 PLYMOUTH ACCLAIM, 6 CYL, TAG:G10–21105, EST MI: 67,705, VIN:1P3XA4637PF623935. (479A654208 #1455)

009 **UTILITY MAINT:** 1987 DODGE DAKOTA, 6 CYL, TAG:G41–74947, EST MI: 33,252, VIN:1B7GN14M5HS486470. (479A654208 #1402)

010 **PICKUP:** 1987 CHEVROLET CR20943, CREW CAB, 8 CYL, TAG:G43–35295, EST MI: 32,106, VIN:1GCGR23K6HS156668. (479A654208 #1403)

011 **PICKUP:** 1991 CHEVROLET C3500,4X4 CREW CAB, 8 CYL, TAG:G63–17713, EST MI: 65,665, DUAL REAR WHEELS, DUAL FUEL TANKS, STD TRANS. W/ CAMPER SHELL, VIN:1GCHV33K5MF304883.(479A654208 #1404)

012 **PASS UTILITY:** 1991 DODGE CARAVAN, 7 PASS. 6 CYL, TAG:G41–86636, EST MI: 74,963,VIN:1B4GK44R1MX561617. (479A654208 #1405)

013 **VAN:** 1987 DODGE B–250, 8CYL, 8 PASS. TAG:G42–46976, EST MI: 47,794, VIN:2B4HB21T6HK258810. (479A654208 #1406)

014 **SEDAN:** 1990 CHEVROLET CORSICA, 6 CYL, TAG:G12–73644, EST MI: 12,619, VIN:1G1LT54T0LE183292. (479A654208 #1407)

015 **SEDAN:** 1990 CHEVROLET CORSICA, 4 CYL, TAG:G12–73690, EST MI: 21,993, VIN:1G1LT54G7LY213082. (479A654208 #1408)

016 **PASS UTILITY:** 1991 CHEVROLET BLAZER, 8 CYL, TAG:G62–17988, EST MI: 81,011, VIN:1GNEV18K0MF135668. (479A654208 #1409)

017 **UTILITY MAINT:** 1988 DODGE DAKOTA, 6 CYL, TAG:G41–75925, EST MI: 48,468, VIN:1B7GN14X2JS726705. (479A654208 #1410)

018 **SEDAN:** 1993 PLYMOUTH ACCLAIM, 6 CYL, TAG:G10–21101, EST MI: 75,433, VIN:1P3XA463XPF623931. (479A654208 #1411)

019 **UTILITY MAINT:** 1987 DODGE DAKOTA, 6 CYL, TAG:G41–76008, EST MI: 50,266, VIN:1B7GN14MXHS506714. (479A654208 #1412)

020 **UTILITY MAINT:** 1987 DODGE DAKOTA, 6 CYL, TAG:G41–74948, EST MI: 43,483, VIN:1B7GN14M7HS486468. (479A654208 #1413)

021 **PASS UTILITY:** 1991 DODGE CARAVAN, 7 PASS, 6 CYL, TAG:G41–86707, EST MI: 71,534,VIN:1B4GK44R0MX561611. (479A654208 #1414)

022 **PICKUP:** CREWCAB, 1987 CHEVROLET FLEETSIDE, 4X4, 8 CYL, TAG:G63–12760, EST MI: 35,511, VIN:1GCHV33K7HS155812.(479A654208 #1415)

023 **PICKUP:** 1987 CHEVROLET S–10, 6 CYL, TAG:G40–02907, EST MI: 34,821, VIN:1GCCS14R0H8194015. (479A654208 #1416)

024 **SEDAN:** 1990 CHEVROLET CORSICA, 4 CYL, TAG:G12–73660, EST MI: 11,250, VIN:1G1LT54G2LY211465. (479A654208 #1417)

025 **UTILITY MAINT:** 1987 DODGE D250, 8 CYL, TAG:G43–35296, EST MI: 62,203, VIN:1B7KD2416HS445144. (479A654208 #1418)

026 **PICKUP:** CREW CAB, 1987 CHEVROLET C30,4X4, 8 CYL, TAG:G63–12745, EST MI: 53,791, VIN:1GCHV33K4HS155783. (479A654208 #1419)

027 **UTILITY MAINT:** 1987 DODGE D250, 8 CYL, TAG:G43–35694, EST MI: 35,026, VIN:1B7KD2413HS500214. (479A654208 #1420)

028 **SEDAN:** 1993 PLYMOUTH ACCLAIM,6 CYL, 6 CYL, TAG:G10–21107, EST MI: 77,133, VIN:1P3XA4630PF623937. (479A654208 #1421)

029 **UTILITY MAINT:** 1987 DODGE D250, 8 CYL, TAG:G43–35299, EST MI: 49,423, VIN:1B7KD2412HS445142. (479A654208 #1422)

030 **UTILITY MAINT:** 1988 DODGE DAKOTA, 6 CYL,TAG:G41–79051, EST MI: 45,049, VIN:1B7GN14X4JS725345. (479A654208 #1423)

031 **UTILITY MAINT:** 1987 DODGE W250, 4X4, 8 CYL, TAG:G63–13198, EST MI: 47,608, VIN:1B7KW2413HS416579. (479A654208 #1424)

032 **VAN:** 15 PASS, 1988 DODGE B350, 8 CYL, TAG:G43–37658, EST MI: 36,284, VIN:2B5WB3118JK131621. (479A6542081 #1425)

033 **UTILITY MAINT:** 1988 DODGE D350, 8 CYL, TAG:G43–37645, EST MI: 56,117, VIN:1B7KD3413JS689457. (479A654208 #1458)

034 **PICKUP:** 1986 DODGE D50, 4 CYL, W/CAMPER SHELL, TAG:G41–10340, EST MI: 40,757, ENGINE NEEDS REPAIRS, VIN:JB7FP44E4GP010700. (479A654208 #1426)

035 **PICKUP:** 1990 DODGE DAKOTA, 6CYL, TAG:G41–85691, EST MI: 33,131, VIN:1B7GL26X6LS752414. ACCIDENT DAMAGE, TOTALLED. (479A654208 #1427)

036 **LIGHT TRUCK:** 4X2, 1987 DODGE D250, S & P, 8 CYL, TAG:G43–35175, EST MI: 44,622, VIN:1B7KD2411HS465575. (479A654208 #1428)

037 **UTILITY MAINT:** 1987 DODGE DAKOTA, 6 CYL,TAG:G41–75905, EST MI: 49,061, VIN:1B7GN14MOHS483430. (479A654208 #1429)

038 **UTILITY MAINT:** 1987 DODGE D250, 8 CYL, TAG:G43–35274, EST MI: 41,861, VIN:1B7KD2411HS450316. (479A654208 #1430)

039 **PICKUP:** 1987 DODGE D150, 6 CYL, TAG:G41–75065, EST MI: 56,675, VIN:1B7GD14H5HS442880. (479A654208 #1454)

040 **PASS UTILITY:** 1991 DODGE CARAVAN, 7 PASS. 6 CYL, TAG:G41–86641, EST MI: 65,055, VIN:1B4GK44R0MX561592.(479A654208 #1431)

041 **UTILITY MAINT:** 1988 DODGE DAKOTA, 6 CYL,TAG:G41–79054, EST MI: 50,615, VIN:1B7GN14X6JS725346. (479A654208 #1432)

042 **UTILITY MAINT:** 1988 DODGE D350, 8 CYL, TAG:G43–37648, EST MI: 48,735, VIN:1B7KD3416JS682051. (479A654208 #1456)

043 **PICKUP:** 1987 DODGE D150, 6 CYL, TAG:G41–74926, EST MI: 42,834, VIN:1B7GD14H9HS442879. (479A654208 #1433)

044 **SEDAN:** 1990 CHEVROLET CORSICA, 6 CYL, TAG:G12–73641, EST MI: 13,095, VIN:1G1LT54T7LE183208. (479A654208 #1434)

045 **PICKUP:** 1987 DODGE D150, 6 CYL, TAG:G41–75100, EST MI: 51,069, VIN:1B7GD14H0HS441927. (479A654208 #1453)

046 **PICKUP:** 1987 DODGE D–150, 6 CYL, TAG:G41–74587, EST MI: 65,800, VIN:1B7GD14HXHS425380, (479A654208 #1435)

047 **PICKUP:** 1987 DODGE D150, 6 CYL, TAG:G41–74986, EST MI: 37,305, VIN:1B7GD14HXHS441921. (479A654208 #1436)

048 **PICKUP:** 1987 DODGE D150, 6 CYL, TAG:G41–74989, EST MI: 51,847, VIN:1B7GD14H0HS441930. (479A654208 #1437)

049 **PICKUP:** 1987 DODGE D150, 6 CYL, TAG:G41–75058, EST MI: 35,258, VIN:1B7GD14H1HS441919. (479A654208 #1438)

050 **PICKUP:** 1987 DODGE D150, 6 CYL, TAG:G41–75064, EST MI: 43,365, VIN:1B7GD14H4HS441932. (479A654208 #1439)

051 **TRUCK:** 1986 INTERNATL'S–1800, FUEL:DIESEL, 4X4, 8 CYL, TAG:G81–04108, EST MI: 35,509, VIN:1HTLFHWL2GHA24687. (479A654208 #1440)

052 **CARGO VAN:** 1983 FORD E–150, 6 CYL, TAG:G42–67907, EST MI: 38,539, VIN:1FTEE14Y50HB48519. (479A654208 #1441)

053 **TRUCK:** 1982 INTERNATL' S1700, VAN BODY, DIESEL, 8 CYL, TAG:G71–15591, ESTMI: 45,747, VIN:1HTAA17E7CHB10614.(479A654208 #1442)

055 **PASS UTILITY:** 1988 CHEVROLET ASTROVAN, 8 PASS, 8 CYL, TAG:G41–79059, EST MI: 47,671, VIN:1GNDM15Z4JB187971.(479A654208 #1444)

056 **PICKUP:** CREWCAB, 1987 CHEVROLET 4X4, 8CYL, TAG:G63–12752, EST MI: 60,173, VIN:1GCHV33K4HS155878. DUAL FUEL TANKS. (479A654208 #1443)

057 **PICKUP:** 1988 CHEVROLET CH2500, 8 CYL, TAG:G43–39526, EST MI: 42,305, VIN:1GCFC24H0JZ226873. (479A654208 #1446)

058 **CARGO VAN:** 1988 CHEVROLET C 30, CUTOFF, 8 CYL, TAG:G43–37718, EST MI: 42,502, VIN:2GCHG31K8J4145453. DUAL REAR WHEELS, (479A654208 #1447)

059 **UTILITY MAINT:** 1987 DODGE D250, 8 CYL, TAG:G43–35269, EST MI: 52,117, VIN:1B7KD2410HS445141. (479A654208 #1457)

060 **PICKUP:** 1988 CHEVROLET 2500, 8 CYL, TAG:G43–38677, EST MI: 31,410, VIN:1GCFC24H3JZ226155. (479A654208 #1448)

061 **PICKUP:** 1987 CHEVROLET CREWCAB, 4X4, 8CYL, TAG:G63–12741, EST MI: 55,827, VIN:1GCHV33K8HS155818. DUAL FUEL TANKS, (479A654208 #1449)

062 **PASS UTILITY:** 1991 DODGE CARAVAN, 7 PASS. 6 CYL, TAG:G41–86645, EST MI: 65,445,VIN:1B4GK44R1MX561598. (479A654208 #1450)

063 **PASS VAN:** 1987 DODGE B350, 12 PASS, 8 CYL,TAG:G43–35276, EST MI: 31,280, VIN:2B5WB31T6HK278306. (479A654208 #1451)

064 **CARAVAN:** 1991 DODGE, 6 CYL, 7 PASS, ALL WHEEL DRIVE, TAG:G61–21968, EST MI: 55,823, VIN:1B4GD44R9MX580233. (479A654208 #1452)

General Services Administration Real Property

The General Services Administration also sells real estate that is no longer needed by the Federal government. The GSA sells property in all 50 states, the District of Columbia, the Virgin Islands, Puerto Rico and the U.S. Pacific territories.

The types of property offered by the GSA can vary widely, from office buildings to parcels of unimproved land. They can also range from former military buildings to commercial property. The GSA is required by law to obtain fair market value for the property it offers at auction. As a general rule, the major properties are offered at auction and the less expensive properties are sold through sealed bid sales. In both cases the bidders are required to place a bid deposit. For the sealed bid sales bidders are required to use a special bidding form available from one of the GSAís four regional sales offices or two field offices. For information about property being offered in the area you are interested in, contact the appropriate regional office as listed below. There are also two field offices that you can contact for additional information.

FOR THE FOLLOWING STATES:

Connecticut, Indiana, Illinois, Maine, Massachusetts, Michigan, Minnesota, New Hampshire, New Jersey, New York, Ohio, Rhode Island, Vermont, Wisconsin, Puerto Rico and the Virgin Islands, contact:

Office of Real Estate Sales (2DR-1)
U.S. General Services Administration
10 Causeway Street
Boston, MA 02222
(617) 565-5700

FOR THE FOLLOWING STATES:

Alabama, Delaware, District of Columbia, Florida, Georgia, Kentucky, Maryland, Mississippi, North Carolina, Pennsylvania, South Carolina, Virginia and West Virginia, contact:

Office of Real Estate Sales (4DR)
U.S. General Services Administration
Peachtree Summit Building
401 West Peachtree Street
Atlanta, GA 30365-2550
(404) 331-5133

FOR THE FOLLOWING STATES:

Arkansas, Colorado, Iowa, Kansas, Louisiana, Missouri, Montana, Nebraska, New Mexico, North Dakota, Oklahoma, South Dakota, Texas, Utah, and Wyoming, contact:

Office of Real Estate Sales (7DR)
U.S. General Services Administration
819 Taylor Street
Ft. Worth, TX 76102
(817) 334-2331

FOR THE FOLLOWING STATES:

Alaska, Arizona, California, Hawaii, Idaho, Nevada, Oregon, Washington, and Guam, contact:

Office of Real Estate Sales (9DR)
U.S. General Services Administration
525 Market Street
San Francisco, CA 94105

Field Offices:

Office of Real Estate Sales (2DRF-5)
U.S. General Services Administration
230 S. Dearborn Street, Room 3864
Chicago, IL 60604
(312) 353-6045

Office of Real Estate Sales (9DR-F)
U.S. General Services Administration
400 15th Street, SW, Room 1138
Auburn, WA 98001-6599
(206) 931-7547

Federal Information Center

Another service offered by the General Services Administration (GSA) is through the Federal Information Center (FIC). If you are having difficulty locating the local offices for a particular sales program, the Federal Information Center can help you. The FIC can tell you the location of the sales office nearest you. You can call the telephone number(s) listed below for your state or area. Please note that the toll-free numbers can only be called within the states and cities listed. If your area is not listed you can call the FIC at:

Federal Information Center
(800) 688-9889

Federal Information Center (FIC) Telephone Numbers

Alabama:
Birmingham, Mobile
1-800-366-2998

Alaska:
Anchorage
1-800-729-8003

Arizona:
Phoenix
1-800-359-3997

Arkansas:
Little Rock
1-800-366-2998

California:
Los Angeles, San Diego, San Francisco, Santa Ana
1-800-726-4995

Sacramento
(916) 973-1695

Colorado:
Colorado Springs, Denver, Pueblo
1-800-359-3997

Connecticut:
Hartford, New Haven
1-800-347-1997

Florida:
Ft. Lauderdale, Miami, Orlando, Jacksonville, St. Petersburg,
Tampa, West Palm Beach
1-800-347-1997

Georgia:
Atlanta
1-800-347-1997

Hawaii:
Honolulu
1-800-733-5996

Illinois:
Chicago
1-800-366-2998

Indiana:
Gary
1-800-366-2998

Indianapolis
1-800-347-1997

Iowa:
All locations
1-800-735-8004

Kansas:
All locations
1-800-735-8004

Kentucky:
Louisville
1-800-347-1997

Louisiana:
New Orleans
1-800-366-2998

Maryland:
Baltimore
1-800-347-1997

Massachusetts:
Boston
1-800-347-1997

Michigan:
Detroit, Grand Rapids
1-800-347-1997

Minnesota:
Minneapolis
1-800-366-2998

Missouri:
St. Louis
1-800-366-2998
All other locations
1-800-735-8004

Nebraska:
Omaha
1-800-366-2998
All other locations
1-800-735-8004

New Jersey:
Newark, Trenton
1-800-347-1997

New Mexico:
Albuquerque
1-800-359-3997

New York:
Albany, Buffalo, New York, Rochester, Syracuse
1-800-347-1997

North Carolina:
Charlotte
1-800-347-1997

Ohio:
Akron, Cincinnati, Cleveland, Columbus, Dayton, Toledo
1-800-688-9889

Oklahoma:
Oklahoma City, Tulsa
1-800-366-2998

Oregon:
Portland
1-800-726-4995

Pennsylvania:
Philadelphia, Pittsburgh
1-800-347-1997

Rhode Island:
Providence
1-800-347-1997

Tennessee:
Chattanooga
1-800-347-1997
Memphis, Nashville
1-800-366-2998

Texas:
Austin, Dallas, Ft. Worth, Houston, San Antonio
1-800-366-2998

Utah:
Salt Lake City
1-800-359-3997

Virginia:
Norfolk, Richmond, Roanoke
1-800-347-1997

Washington:
Seattle, Tacoma
1-800-726-4995

Wisconsin:
All locations
1-800-366-2998

Again, if your area is not listed above, call the Federal Information Center at (800) 688-9889.

Chapter 14:
Department of Defense

"I saw a DRMO Successful Bidder's List and People were getting deals I couldn't believe. One guy had bought a 4-ton hydraulic jack for only $40.00. Someone else had bought a 1992 Ford Sedan for just $650.00. Pick-ups were going for $450.00. There was everything from office furniture and equipment to satellite dishes and galley equipment, and everything went at bargain prices."

T. Hickey

Department of Defense auctions are some of the most popular. In fact, other than the U.S. Trustees auctions, IRS and Customs auctions, these are probably your next best source of bargains! And since your tax dollars paid for the items being auctioned off in the first place, you should feel really good when you are able to get a great deal! The Pentagon may spend $150,000 on a new computer system, while their DRMOs are selling off their "old" equipment for $10 to $20. You'd be hard pressed to find a bargain like that at WalMart!

The Department of Defense sells military surplus property that has been released by the Army, Air Force, Marine Corps and Navy. To receive mailing list information, write them at the following address:

Department of Defense
Defense Property Disposal Service
Federal Center
74 N. Washington
Battle Creek, MI 49017-3092

The National Sales Office shown on the following page is currently the consolidated sales office that conducts National sales of Department of Defense surplus property. This office prepares sales catalogs, administers bid openings, and makes awards.

In order to get on the mailing list to receive National sales catalogs, you must complete an application. This will place your name on the National Bidders list, which records the geographical location(s) and class(es) of property you are interested in purchasing. When there is a class of property you are interested in obtaining available in the geographical location you noted, you will receive a sales catalog. The catalog advises you of the types of property for sale, location, and dates. Figure 3 on pages 197-198 at the end of this directory shows what this Surplus Property Bidders Application looks like. Contact the office at the address below to request a Surplus Property Bidders Application.

Defense Reutilization and Marketing Service
National Sales Office
P.O. Box 5275 DDRC
2163 Airways Blvd.
Memphis, TN 38114-5210
1-800-468-8289

The Pacific division offices also maintain a bidders list for sales of property held within its geographic area. To be placed on that list, contact:

Pacific Division Office
Bldg. 12
Camp H.M. Smith, HI 96861-5010
(808) 477-1227

As a general rule, your name will be removed from the mailing lists if you fail to bid after receipt of at least five catalogs.

Defense Logistics Agency, Defense Reutilization and Marketing Service

The Defense Reutilization and Marketing Service (DRMS) of the Defense Logistics Agency is responsible for managing the Department of Defense (DoD) Government Sales Program. Excess personal property from U.S. military units is turned over to more than 200 Defense Reutilization and Marketing Offices (DRMOs) located on major military installations around the world. The property is first looked at for reutilization or reuse within the DoD. When property cannot be reused, it is offered for transfer or donation to other federal agencies and qualified state and local agencies. The remaining property is declared surplus and offered for sale to the public.

Property varies in type and value and includes vehicles, aircraft components, engine accessories, computers, typewriters, office furniture and equipment, tents, clothing, household paints and thinners, recyclable materials such as iron, aluminum, copper, paper, and much more. DRMS does not sell real estate.

Local sales are held at DRMOs either by auction or spot bid. Property may be inspected prior to the sale. Most DRMOs have regularly scheduled sales and set times. Some DRMOs have cash and carry sales, where small quantities of individual items are offered at a fixed price based on current market value.

National sales are conducted by the National Sales Office in Memphis, Tennessee. The property offered through national sales includes items such as aircraft, ships, hazardous property and property having commercial application. National sales methods are sealed bids, auction, and in some circumstances, negotiated sales.

Local sales are conducted by individual DRMOs and are advertised locally in the print media, television, radio and fliers. National sales are conducted by the National Sales Office and advertised in the Commerce Business Daily, trade publications and papers that target specialized markets. To participate, you must be at least 18 years old. Employees of DRMS, their agents and members of their households cannot buy property.

Property is offered for sale "as is/where is." Buyers of hazardous property such as paints, solvents and oils must demonstrate and certify that they are environmentally responsible and that they possess the necessary licenses and permits to transport, handle or store hazardous property.

GOVERNMENT SURPLUS SALE

CONDUCTED BY DRMO II YUMA ARIZONA

OFFERING:

TYPEWRITERS, COMPUTERS, OFFICE EQUIPMENT, COPIERS, PUMPS, REFRIGERATORS,
GENERATORS, FURNITURE, CARS, TRUCKS, WASHERS, DRYERS, TIRES, TOOLS,
AIR CONDITIONERS AND MUCH, MUCH, MORE.

NOTE: Item locations are listed inside catalog for your convenience.

NOTE: PLEASE BRING THIS CATALOG TO THE SALE SITE WHEN INSPECTING.

NOTE: Please call

Office Hours 7:00 AM to 3:30 PM

***   NO PHONE INQUIRES PRIOR TO FIRST DAY OF INSPECTION THANK YOU. ***

I HAVE PHYSICALLY REVIEWED THIS PROPERTY, AND TO THE BEST OF MY KNOWLEDGE
THIS SALE CONTAINS NO MLI/SLI PROPERTY.

DRMO II YUMA

****

INSPECTION/REMOVAL TIMES 0730-1430***FINAL REMOVAL DATE IS 21 DECEMBER

****

DATE AND TIME: 12/14 08:00 AM	**SALE NUMBER:** 41-5604
REGISTRATION: 07:30 AM	**SALE SITE:** SHILO INN HOTEL, YUMA BLDG :TUCSON ROOM
CONTACT: SHIRLEY OR TRACY	**METHOD:** AUCTION

INSPECTION:
12/09   to 12/13   07:30 TO 14:30

(excluding weekends and holidays)

Guaranteed payment such as cashier's check or certified check is required. There are some instances where credit cards can be used.

These are **GREAT** auctions to go to. At both local DRMO and DRMR, we surplus buyers can expect to immediately **TRIPLE** our investment. There are times when individuals make as much as ten times what they invested. These opinions are the consensus we've found in talking with and interviewing auctioneers and surplus buyers who make a living doing just what you want to do. Visit an auction and you'll likely hear stories even more astounding than this.

Hard to find materials are often available at these auctions. Equipment sells for next to nothing. It's not uncommon for trucks to sell for a few hundred dollars. DRMRs often underestimate the resale value of the merchandise and equipment they handle. Their appraisals are very often less than accurate. Because of this, these auctions can be a great way to make a substantial profit.

If you're looking for a vehicle, these auctions may be just your ticket! The prices are unbelievable. Are you ready for a few examples to whet your appetite? How about a 1971 Fiat Spider Convertible for $35? Or maybe you'd like to bid on a 1976 VW Rabbit at $55. Toyota Celicas and Tercels often sell for under $100. A 1976 Dodge Sports Van sold for just $150.

If you're not interested in a car, perhaps you would be interested in a Canon copier for $20, or maybe a FAX machine for just $25? Color television sets have gone for only $35, and 2 Johnson outboard motors were purchased for a mere $235.

When you consider how often these auctions take place, it's easy to see that it's pretty simple to find bargains if you attend.

On the following pages, you'll find a listing of the various numbers and addresses for the DRMS, DRMR and DRMOs around the world. Contact the ones you're interested in and have them start sending you notices about upcoming auctions!

Defense Reutilization and Marketing Offices (DRMOs)

Alabama:

DRMO - Anniston (EAST)
Anniston Army Depot
Anniston, AL 36201-5090
(205) 235-7733, 235-7133

DRMO - Montgomery (EAST)
Gunter AFS, 900
Montgomery, AL 36114-5000
(334) 416-4194

DRMO - Huntsville (EAST)
Bldg. 7408
Redstone Arsenal, AL 35898-7230
(205) 955-2570

DRMO - Rucker (EAST)
Ft. Rucker, AL 36362-5286
(334) 255-1213

Alaska:

DRMO - Anchorage (WEST)
P.O. Box 166, Bldg. 34-600
Elmendorf AFB, AK 99506-0166
(907) 552-3733

DRMO - Fairbanks (WEST)
P.O. Box 35028
Ft. Wainwright, AK 99703-0028
(907) 353-7130

Arizona:

DRMO - Luke (WEST)
7011 North El Mirage Rd.
Luke AFB
Glendale, AZ 85307-5000
(602) 856-7144

DRMO - Tuscon (WEST)
Davis-Monthan AFB
Tucson, AZ 85708-0011
(602) 750-3819
(520) 225-8818

Arkansas:

DRMO - Little Rock (WEST)
Little Rock AFB
Bldg. 1575
Jacksonville, AR 72099-5094
(501) 988-3363

California:

DRMO - Alameda (WEST)
2155 Mariner Square Loop
Bldg. 4
Alameda, CA 94501-1022
(510) 869-8283

DRMO - Barstow (WEST)
Marine Corps Logistics Base
Box 110195
Barstow, CA 92311-5037
(619) 577-6567, 577-6568

DRMO - El Toro (WEST)
P.O. Box 21
East Irvine, CA 92650-0021
(714) 726-4937

DRMO - McClellan (WEST)
Bldg. 700-A
McClellan AFB, CA 95652-6448
(916) 643-2061

DRMO - Norton (WEST)
Bldg. 948
March AFB, CA 92409-6488
(909) 655-7134

DRMO - Pendelton (WEST)
P.O. Box 1608
Oceanside, CA 92051-1608
(619) 725-3605, 725-4332

DRMO - Port Hueneme (WEST)
NCBC, Bldg. 513
Port Hueneme, CA 93043-5015
(805) 982-5646

DRMO - San Diego (WEST)
P.O. Box 337
Imperial Beach, CA 91933-0337
(619) 437-9446

DRMO - Stockton (WEST)
Rough and Ready Island
Bldg. 1002
Stockton, CA 95203-4901
(209) 944-0291

Connecticut:

DRMO - Groton (EAST)
Naval Submarine Base
New London
Box 12
Groton, CT 06349-5012
(203) 449-3524

Delaware:

DRMO - Dover (EAST)
Bldg. 114
Dover AFB, DE 19902-5639
(302) 677-3201

Florida:

DRMO - Eglin (EAST)
210 Transportation Rd., Suite 1
Eglin AFB, FL 32542-5212
(904) 882-2822, 882-2823

DRMO - Jacksonville (EAST)
P.O. Box 82
Jacksonville, FL 32212-0082
(904) 772-3411, 772-3412

DRMO - Key West (EAST)
NAS Harry S. Truman Annex
Bldg. 795, P.O. Box 1938
Key West, FL 33041-1938
(305) 293-5271, 298-5272

DRMO - Patrick (EAST)
1391 Marina Rd.
Patrick AFB, FL 32925-7469
(407) 494-6507

DRMO - Pensacola (EAST)
U.S. Naval Air Station
260 Warehouse Rd., Suite A
Pensacola, FL 32508
(904) 452-2451, 452-2452

Panama:

DRMO - Panama (EAST)
APO Miami 34002-5000
(313) 285-4754

Georgia:

DRMO - Albany (EAST)
Marine Corps Logistics Base
P.O. Box 43139
Albany, GA 31704
(912) 439-5967

DRMO - Stewart (EAST)
Bldg. 1152
Ft. Stewart, GA 31314
(912) 767-8863, 767-8878

DRMO - Warner-Robins (EAST)
1200 Macon St.
Robins AFB, GA 31098-2502
(912) 926-3437, 926-2387

Greenland:

DRMO - Thule (EAST)
Thule Air Base
APO, NY 09121-5000
Phone: none

Hawaii:

DRMO - Hawaii (WEST)
Box 580
Pearl City, HI 96782-0580
(808) 684-5870

Idaho:

None

Illinois:

DRMO - Great Lakes (EAST)
Naval Training Ctr., Bldg. 3212A
Great Lakes, IL 60088-5798
(708) 688-3655, 688-3656

DRMO - Rock Island (EAST)
Rock Island Arsenal, Bldg. 154
Rock Island, IL 61299-7030
(309) 782-1617

DRMO - Scott (EAST)
Bldg. 4141
Scott AFB, IL 62225-5000
(618) 256-5964

Indiana:

DRMO - Crane (EAST)
Naval Weapons Support Center
Crane, IN 47522-5091
(812) 854-1728

Iowa:

None

Kansas:

DRMO - Riley (WEST)
P.O. Box 2490
Ft. Riley, KS 66442-2490
(913) 239-6202, 239-6203

Kentucky:

DRMO - Campbell (EAST)
P.O. Box 555
Ft. Campbell, KY 42223-0555
(502) 798-4897, 798-3525

DRMO - Knox (EAST)
Bldg. 2962 Frazier Road
Ft. Knox, KY 40121-5640
(502) 624-1328, 624-5255

DRMO - Lexington (EAST)
Lexington-Blue Grass Army Depot
Lexington, KY 40511-5108
(606) 625-6678

Louisiana:

DRMO - Barksdale (WEST)
1264 Twining
Barksdale AFB, LA 71110
(318) 454-8650

DRMO - Polk (WEST)
P.O. Drawer 3901
Ft. Polk, LA 71459-0901
(318) 531-4068, 531-4064

Maine:

DRMO - Brunswick (EAST)
Naval Air Station, Bldg. 584
Brunswick, ME 04011-5000
(207) 921-2627, 921-2452

Maryland:

DRMO - Aberdeen (EAST)
Aberdeen Proving Ground
Bldg. 3620
Aberdeen, MD 21005-5001
(410) 278-2235, 278-4785

Massachusetts:

DRMO -Westover (EAST)
Bldg. 1604
Westover AFB, MA 01022-5000
(410) 557-3939

Michigan:

DRMO - Selfridge (EAST)
Bldg. 590
Selfridge ANG Base, MI 48045-5003
(810) 307-4586, 307-5191, 307-4806

Minnesota:

DRMO - Duluth (EAST)
c/o 148th Fighter Interceptor Gp
Minnesota ANG
Duluth International Airport
Duluth, MN 55811-5000
(218) 723-7441

Mississippi

DRMO - Keesler (EAST)
607 Parade Ln.
Keesler AFB, MS 39534-2045
(601) 377-3327, 377-2393

Missouri:

DRMO - Whiteman (WEST)
P.O. Box 6010
Whiteman AFB, MO 65305-6100
(816) 687-3308

Montana:

DRMO - Great Falls (WEST)
8035 Pole Yard Rd.
Malmstrom AFB, MT 59402-6807
(406) 731-6346, 731-6348

Nebraska:

DRMO - Offutt (WEST)
P.O. Box 13292
Omaha, NE 68113-6100
(402) 294-3934, 294-4964
FAX: (402) 294-2698

Nevada:

DRMO - Las Vegas
5506 Blightville Dr.
Las Vegas, NV 89191-6216
(702) 652-2004

New Hampshire:

DRMO - Portsmouth (EAST)
Portsmouth Naval Shipyard
P.O. Box 2028
Portsmouth, NH 03801-2028
(207) 438-5154

New Jersey:

DRMO - Lakehurst (EAST)
Naval Air Engineering Ctr.
Bldg. 75
Lakehurst, NJ 08733-5010
(908) 323-2691

New Mexico:

DRMO - Cannon (WEST)
Bldg. 215
Cannon AFB, NM 88103-5000
(505) 784-2437

DRMO - Kirtland (WEST)
Bldg.1025
Kirtland AFB, NM 87117-6100
(505) 846-6959

New York:

DRMO - Plattsburgh (EAST)
P.O. Box 864
Plattsburgh AFB, NY 12901-0864
(518) 565-5779

DRMO - Watervliet (EAST)
Watervliet Arsenal, Bldg. 145
Watervliet, NY 12189-4050

North Carolina:

DRMO - Bragg (EAST)
Bldg. 1334, Knox St.
Ft. Bragg, NC 28307-5000
(910) 396-5298, 396-5222

DRMO - Cherry Point (EAST)
PSC 4298, MCAS
Cherry Point, NC 28533-4298
(919) 466-2743, 466-5905

North Dakota:

DRMO - Grand Forks (WEST)
548 3rd Ave.
Grand Forks AFB
Grand Forks, ND 58205-6032
(701) 747-3783

DRMO - Minot (WEST)
401 Bomber Blvd.
Minot AFB, ND 58705-5010
(701) 723-3241

Ohio:

DRMO - Columbus (EAST)
P.O. Box 13297
Columbus, OH 43213-0297
(614) 692-3244, 692-2316

DRMO - Wright-Patterson (EAST)
Bldg. 89, Area C
Wright-Patterson AFB
OH 45433-5000
(513) 257-4203, 257-7823

Oklahoma:

DRMO - Oklahoma City (WEST)
Tinker AFB / L-11
Oklahoma City, OK 73145-5000
(405) 739-7885

DRMO - Sill (WEST)
Bldg. 3323
Ft. Sill, OK 73503-6900
(405) 442-4703, 442-2918

Oregon:

None

Pennsylvania:

DRMO - Chambersburg (EAST)
Letterkenny Army Depot
P.O. Box 229
Chambersburg, PA 17201-0229
(717) 267-5425

DRMO - Mechanicsburg (EAST)
Nacy SPCC Mechanicsburg
Bldg. 206
5450 Carlisle Pike
P.O. Box 2020
Mechanicsburg, PA 17055-0788
(717) 790-3325
(717) 790-2207

DRMO - Philadelphia (EAST)
2800 S. 20th St.
Bldg. 26-C
Philadelphia, PA 19101-8419
(215) 737-3720, 737-3721

Puerto Rico:

DRMO - Roosevelt Roads (EAST)
PSC 1080, Bldg. 1973
FPO Miami 34051
(809) 865-4903

South Carolina:

DRMO - Charleston (EAST)
P.O. Box 5715
North Charleston, SC 29408-0715
(803) 743-5319, 743-3008

DRMO - Jackson (EAST)
Bldg. 1902
Ft. Jackson, SC 29207-6050
(803) 751-7912, 751-7716

South Dakota:

DRMO - Ellsworth (WEST)
650 Twinings
Ellsworth AFB
Rapid City, SD 57706-4920
(605) 385-1018 - Central
(605) 385-1021 - Auctions

Tennessee:

DRMO - Memphis (WEST)
2163 Airways Blvd.
Memphis, TN 38114-5052
(901) 775-4895

Texas:

DRMO - Bliss (WEST)
1733 Pleasanton
El Paso, TX 79916-0058
(915) 568-8503, 568-8208

DRMO - Corpus Christi (WEST)
NAS, Bldg. 22
Corpus Christi, TX 78419-5600
(512) 939-3359

DRMO - Dyess (WEST)
P.O. Box 9545
Dyess AFB, TX 79607-6100
(915) 696-5287

DRMO - Hood (WEST)
80th Street
P.O. Drawer G
Ft. Hood, TX 76544-0210
(817) 287-5616

DRMO - San Antonio
Bldg. 3050, E. Kelly
Kelly AFB, TX 78241-5000
(512) 925-6167, 925-6168
(210) 925-7766

DRMO - Sheppard (WEST)
DRMO/37 Bldg. 2135
Sheppard AFB, TX 76311-5000
(817) 676-4933, 676-4934

DRMO - Texarkana (WEST)
P.O. Box 1330
Hooks, TX 75561-1330
(903) 334-3178

Utah:

DRMO - Hill (WEST)
7544 Arsenal Rd.
Bldg. 890
Hill AFB, UT 84056-5000
(801) 777-7422, 777-6659
(801) 777-6557 Auction

Vermont:

None

Virginia:

DRMO - Belvoir (EAST)
M/S 566/SX151 W
Bldg. 2517
Ft. Belvoir, VA 22060-5566
(703) 806-5632

DRMO - Norfolk (EAST)
Norfolk Naval Station Post Office
P.O. Box 15068
Norfolk, VA 23511-0068
(804) 444-5744, 444-5222, 444-5826

DRMO - Richmond (EAST)
Defense General Supply Ctr.
Warehouse 3
8000 Jefferson Davis Hwy.
Richmond, VA 23297-5000
(804) 279-4325

DRMO - Williamsburg (EAST)
Cheatham Annex
Bldg. 16
Naval Supply Center
Williamsburg, VA 23187-8792
(804) 887-7264, 887-7164

Washington:

DRMO - Lewis (WEST)
MS 41, Box 339500
Fort Lewis, WA 98433-9500
(206) 967-7861

West Virginia:

None

Wisconsin:

DRMO - Sparta (EAST)
2184 South 8th Ave.
Sparta, WI 54656-5000
(608) 388-3719, 388-3718

Wyoming:

None

Chapter 15:
SBA Auctions

> "I've been attending auctions for about 9 months. I'm in the process of trying to establish a business buying and selling items. You should always be buying at 25 cents on the dollar or less. I sell computers, nuts, bolts, etc. Some of the stuff is worth thousands and thousands of dollars! I've found the closer you get to a big city, the higher the prices go."
>
> J. Frank

The SBA (Small Business Administration) was created to assist small businesses in getting off the ground. The majority of SBA loans go through banks. Through the SBA's Certified or Preferred Lending Plan, designated banks are able to expedite loan requests for small businesses. Additionally, individuals can go directly to the SBA for a loan if they are unable to work something out with their lending institution. The SBA's primary source of merchandise for auction is their loan guarantee program. When a business which has borrowed money from the SBA fails, the collateral the business was forced to pledge to secure the loan is auctioned off by the bank doing the lending.

The SBA doesn't really relish the idea of being in the auction business. They are happier lending money to help start or expand a business.

The SBA actually guarantees the loans that banks give to small businesses — up to 90%. What does this mean to you? Well, if a business goes belly up and owes money due to an SBA loan, the bank is only worried about recouping about 15%, since the SBA will write the bank a check to cover their loss on the remainder.

When a SBA backed company fails, their inventory, equipment and/or real estate is repossessed by the bank. What is usually taken back are hard assets which can easily be sold.

When real estate is involved, the banks often just buy the property at auction (if it is a house or building) and include it in their real estate owned (REO) department as a non-performing asset. Buyers get a second chance to purchase the property, many times for less than the bank paid at the auction for it. You can contact your local bank's real estate owned department to see what they have available to make an offer on. Sometimes, the bank asks the SBA to handle the auction.

When auctions are held by either the bank or the SBA, they are public auctions. This doesn't mean you can't attempt to negotiate a sale with any of the entities involved. Don't ever hesitate to talk to the bank, the SBA or even the auctioneer to see if you can agree on an offer. SBA auctions abide pretty much by the same rules as bankruptcy auctions.

SBA auctions are every bit as enticing as the other auctions you'll be attending. They aren't as organized as the GSA's, so you won't be hindered by firm policies or reserve prices.

You can even find real estate at SBA auctions, because it may have been pledged as collateral. Therefore, you should keep your eyes open for real estate as well as personal property at these auctions.

Items are sold by public auction, sealed bid, sealed bidders auction, listing with brokers or dealers and by private negotiation. Sales are advertised in classified and display ads in local, regional, national and international newspapers. Additionally, they appear in trade and industry publications.

Unless otherwise specified, all sales are "as is." The buyer is responsible for removal. For the most part, only cash or guaranteed payment such as a cashier's check or certified check are accepted. The sales advertisements will provide payment information. The terms and conditions of each sale are read at the start of the sale. All prospective bidders should be present at this time, since bidders are bound by these announcements, and there may be some last minute changes or additions to the advertised terms.

For more information, you can contact your local SBA District Office. To find the district office nearest you, call 1-(800)-827-5722, or look for the Small Business Administration under the "U.S. Government" listings in the telephone directories of the major cities in your state. You can also contact the nearest field office from the list we have provided for you at the end of this chapter. When you call, ask to speak to the Liquidation Chief, and specify the types of assets you wish to buy, the general price range, and the geographic location in which you're interested. To see about being placed on a localized mailing list, contact the SBA Liquidation Chief in the location where you wish to buy goods to see if one is available.

While researching this book, we made an interesting discovery: the Small Business Administration has a database which lists ALL of the assets they currently have available for sale. That's right, a centralized listing of property which will be available for sale. Not only do they list the merchandise, but they provide you with pertinent information about it, as well as a way to reach a contact.

If you have a computer and a modem, you can simply dial 1-(703) 321-8020 to gain access. The FEDWORLD program offers gateway systems for access to the SBA on-line. Talk about getting information straight from the horse's mouth!!

To locate the SBA office nearest you, call **1-800-U-ASK-SBA** (1-800-827-5722). Once you've been connected to your local office, ask for the Liquidations Chief to see if they maintain a mailing list. If they do—get on it!

Small Business Administration Field Locations:

Alabama:

2121 8th Avenue, North
Suite 200
Birmingham, AL 35023-2398
(205) 731-1344
FAX (205) 731-1404

Alaska:

222 West 8th Avenue, Room 67
Anchorage, AK 99513-7559
(907) 271-4022
FAX (907) 271-4545

Arizona:

2828 North Central Avenue
Suite 800
Phoenix, AZ 85004-1093
(602) 640-2316
FAX (602) 640-2360

Arkansas:

2120 Riverfront Dr., Suite 100
Little Rock, AR 72202-1747
(501) 324-5278
FAX (501) 324-5199

California:

2719 N. Air Fresno Drive
Fresno, CA 93727-1547
(209) 487-5189
FAX (209) 487-5636

330 N. Brand Blvd., Suite 1200
Glendale, CA 91203-2304
(213) 894-2956
FAX (213) 894-5665

660 "J" Street, Room 215
Sacramento, CA 95814-2413
(916) 551-1426
FAX (916) 551-1439

1825 Bell Street, Suite 208
Sacramento, CA 95825
(916) 978-4571
FAX (916) 978-4577

880 Front Street, Suite 4-S-29
San Diego, CA 92188-0270
(619) 557-7252
FAX (619) 557-5894

71 Stevenson Street, 20th Floor
San Francisco, CA 94105-2939
(415) 744-6402
FAX (415) 744-6435

211 Main Street, 4th Floor
San Francisco, CA 94105-1988
(415) 744-6820
FAX (415) 744-6812

901 W. Civic Center Dr., Suite 160
Santa Ana, CA 92703-2352
(714) 836-2494
FAX (714) 836-2528

6477 Telephone Road, Suite 10
Ventura, CA 93003-4459
(805) 642-1866
FAX (805) 642-9538

Colorado:

999 18th Street, Suite 701
Denver, CO 80202
(303) 844-0500
FAX (303) 383-5620

721 19th Street, Room 407
Denver, CO 80201-0660
(303) 844-3984
FAX (303) 844-6539

Connecticut:

330 Main Street, 2nd Floor
Hartford, CT 06106
(203) 240-4700
FAX (203) 240-4659

Delaware:

920 N. King Street, Suite 412
Wilmington, DE 19801
(302) 573-6295
FAX (302) 573-6060

District of Columbia

110 Vermont Ave. NW, 9th Floor
Washington, DC 20005
(202) 606-4000
FAX (202) 634-1803

Florida:

1320 S. Dixie Highway, Suite 501
Coral Gables, FL 33146-2911
(305) 536-5521
FAX (305) 536-5058

7825 Baymeadows Way
Suite 100-B
Jacksonville, FL 32256-7504
(904) 443-1900
FAX (904) 443-1980

Georgia:

1375 Peachtree St., NE, Room 500
Atlanta, GA 30309
(404) 347-2797
FAX (404) 347-2355

1720 Peachtree Road, NW
6th Floor
Atlanta, GA 30309
(404) 347-4749
FAX (404) 347-4745

One Baltimore Place, Suite 300
Atlanta, GA 30308
(404) 347-3771
FAX (404) 347-3813

52 North Main Street, Room 225
Statesboro, GA 30458
(912) 489-8719

Guam:

238 Archbishop F.C. Flores St.
Room 508
Agana, GM 96910
(671) 472-7277
FAX (200) 550-7365

Hawaii:

300 Ala Moana Blvd., Room 2213
Honolulu, HI 96850-4981
(808) 541-2990
FAX (808)541-2976

Idaho:

1020 Main Street, Suite 290
Boise, ID 83702-5745
(208) 334-1696
FAX (208) 334-9353

Illinois:

300 S. Riverside Plaza
Suite 1975 S
Chicago, IL 60606-6617
(312) 353-5000
FAX (312) 353-3426

500 W. Madison Street
Room 1250
Chicago, IL 60661-2511
(312) 353-4528
FAX (312) 886-5108

511 W. Capitol Street, Suite 302
Springfield, IL 62704
(217) 492-4416
FAX (217) 492-4867

Indiana:

429 N. Pennsylvania St., Suite 100
Indianapolis, IN 46229
(317) 226-7272
FAX (317) 226-7259

Iowa:

210 Walnut Street, Room 749
Des Moines, IA 50309-2186
(515) 284-4422
FAX (515) 284-4572

Kansas:

100 E. English Street, Suite 510
Wichita, KS 67202
(316) 269-6273
FAX (316) 269-6499

Kentucky:

600 Dr. M.L. King Jr. Place
Room 188
Louisville, KY 40202-2254
(502) 582-5971
FAX (502) 582-5009

Louisiana:

1661 Canal Street, Suite 2000
New Orleans, LA 70112
(504) 589-6685
FAX (504) 589-2339

Maine:

40 Western Ave., Room 512
Augusta, ME 04330
(207) 622-8378
FAX (207) 622-8277

Maryland:

10 S. Howard St.
Baltimore, MD 21201
(410) 962-4392
FAX (410) 962-1805

Massachusetts:

10 Causeway Street, Room 265
Boston, MA 02222-1093
(617) 565-5590
FAX (617) 565-5598

1550 Main Street, Room 212
Springfield, MA 01103
(413) 785-0268
FAX (413) 785-0267

Michigan:

477 Michigan Avenue, Room 515
Detroit, MI 48226
(313) 226-6075
FAX (313) 226-4769

228 W. Washington
Marquette, MI 49855
(906) 225-1108
FAX (906) 225-1109

Minnesota:

100 North 6th Street, Suite 610
Minneapolis, MN 55403-1563
(612) 370-2324
FAX (612) 370-2303

Mississippi:

One Hancock Plaza, Suite 1001
Gulfport, MS 39501-7758
(601) 863-4449
FAX (601) 864-0179

101 W. Capitol Street, Suite 400
Jackson, MS 39201
(601) 965-4378
FAX (601) 965-4294

Missouri:

323 West 8th Street, Suite 501
Kansas City, MO 64105
(816) 374-6708
FAX (816) 374-6759

620 S. Glenstone Street, Suite 110
Springfield, MO 65802-3200
(417) 864-7670
FAX (417) 864-4108

815 Olive Street, Room 242
St. Louis, MO 63101
(314) 539-6600
FAX (314) 539-3785

Montana:

301 South Park, Drawer 10054
Helena, MT 59626
(406) 449-5381
FAX (406) 449-5474

Nebraska:

11145 Mill Valley Road
Omaha, NE 68154
(402) 221-4691
FAX (402) 221-3680

Nevada:

301 E. Stewart Street, Room 301
Las Vegas, NV 89125-2527
(702) 388-6611
FAX (702) 388-6469

New Hampshire:

143 N. Main Street, Suite 202
Concord, NH 03301
(603) 225-1400
FAX (603) 225-1409

New Jersey:

60 Park Place, 4th Floor
Newark, NJ 07201
(201) 645-2434
FAX (201) 645-6265

New Mexico:

625 Silver Ave., SW, Suite 320
Albuquerque, NM 87102
(505) 766-1870
FAX (505) 766-1057

New York:

111 W. Huron Street, Room 1311
Buffalo, NY 14202
(716) 551-4301
FAX (716) 551-4418

333 E. Water Street, 4th Floor
Elmira, NY 14901
(607) 734-8130
FAX (607) 733-4656

35 Pinelawn Road, Room 102E
Melville, NY 11747
(516) 454-0750
FAX (516) 454-0769

360 Rainbow Blvd South, 3rd Floor
Niagara Falls, NY 14303-1192
(716) 282-4612
FAX (716) 282-1472

201 Varrick Street, Room 628
New York, NY 10014
(212) 620-3722
FAX (212) 620-3730

26 Federal Plaza, Room 3108
New York, NY 10278
(212) 264-1450
FAX (212) 264-0900

100 State Street, Room 410
Rochester, NY 14614
(716) 263-6700
FAX (716) 263-3146

100 S. Clinton Street, Room 1071
Syracuse, NY 13260
(315) 423-5383
(315) 423-5370

North Carolina:

200 N. College Street
Charlotte, NC 28202
(704) 344-6563
FAX (704) 344-6769

North Dakota:

657 2nd Avenue, North, Room 219
Fargo, ND 58108-3086
(701) 239-5131
FAX (701) 239-5645

Ohio:

525 Vine Street, Suite 870
Cincinnati, OH 45202
(513) 684-2814
FAX (513) 684-3251

111 Superior, Suite 630
Cleveland, OH 44144
(216) 522-4180
FAX (216) 522-2038

2 Nationwide Plaza, Suite 1400
Columbus, OH 43215-2592
(614) 469-6860
FAX (614) 469-2391

Oklahoma:

200 NW 5th Street, Suite 670
Oklahoma City, OK 73102
(405) 231-4301
FAX (405) 231-4876

Oregon:

222 SW Columbia, Suite 500
Portland, OR 97201-6605
(503) 326-2682
FAX (503) 326-2808

Pennsylvania:

100 Chestnut Street, Room 309
Harrisburg, PA 17101
(717) 782-3840
FAX (717) 782-4839

475 Allendale Road, Suite 201
King of Prussia, PA 19406
(610) 962-3700
FAX (610) 962-3743

960 Penn Avenue, 5th Floor
Pittsburgh, PA 15222
(412) 644-2780
FAX (412) 644-5446

20 N. Pennsylvania Ave.
Room 2327
Wilkes-Barre, PA 18701
(717) 826-6497
FAX (717) 826-6287

Puerto Rico:

Carlos Chardon Ave., Room 691
Hato Rey, PR 00918
(809) 766-5572
FAX (809) 766-5309

Rhode Island:

380 Westminster Street
Providence, RI 02903
(401) 528-4561
FAX (401) 528-4539

South Carolina:

1835 Assembly Street, Room 358
Columbia, SC 29201
(803) 765-5376
FAX (803) 765-5962

South Dakota:

110 S. Phillips, Suite 200
Sioux Falls, SD 57102
(605) 330-4231
FAX (605) 330-4215

Tennessee:

50 Vintage Way, Suite 201
Nashville, TN 37228-1500
(615) 736-5881
FAX (615) 736-7232

Texas:

727 E. Durango, Room A522
San Antonio, TX 78206
(210) 229-5900

606 N. Carancahua, Suite 1200
Corpus Christi, TX 78476
(512) 888-3331
FAX (512) 888-3418

8625 King George Dr., Bldg. C
Dallas, TX 75235-3391
(214) 767-7633
FAX (214) 767-7870

1100 Commerce St., Rm 3C-36
Dallas, TX 75242
(214) 767-0605
FAX (214) 767-0493

10737 Gateway West, Suite 320
El Paso, TX 79935
(915) 540-5676
FAX (915) 540-5636

819 Taylor Street, Room 8A-27
Ft. Worth, TX 76102
(817) 885-6500

4400 Amon Carter Blvd., Suite 102
Ft Worth, TX 76155
(817) 885-7600
FAX (817) 885-7616

222 E. Van Buren Street
Room 500
Harlingen, TX 78550
(210) 427-8533
FAX (210) 427-8537

9301 Southwest Freeway
Suite 550
Houston, TX 77074-1591
(713) 773-6500

1611 Tenth Street, Suite 200
Lubbock, TX 79401-2693
(806) 743-7462
FAX (806) 743-7487

Utah:

125 S. State Street, Room 2237
Salt Lake City, UT 84138-1195
(801) 524-5800
FAX (801) 524-4160

Vermont:

87 State Street, Room 205
Montpelier, VT 05602
(802) 828-4422
FAX (802) 828-4485

Virginia:

1504 Santa Rosa Road
Richmond, VA 23229
(804) 771-2400
FAX (804) 771-8018

Virgin Islands:

4200 United Shopping Plaza
Suite 7
St. Croix, VI 00820-4487
(809) 778-5380
FAX (809) 778-1012

Veterans Drive, Room 210
St. Thomas, VI 00802
(809) 774-8530
FAX (809) 776-2312

Washington:

1200 6th Avenue, Suite 1805
Seattle, WA 98101-1128
(206) 553-5676
FAX (206) 553-4155

West 601 First Avenue
10th Floor E
Spokane, WA 99204-0317
(509) 353-2801
FAX (509) 353-2829

West Virginia:

550 Eagan Street, Room 309
Charleston, WV 25301
(304) 347-5220
FAX (304) 347-5350

168 W. Main Street, 5th Floor
Clarksburg, WV 26301
(304) 623-5631
FAX (304) 623-0023

Wisconsin:

212 E. Washington Avenue
Room 213
Madison, WI 53703
(608) 264-5261
FAX (608) 264-5541

310 W. Wisconsin Avenue
Suite 400
Milwaukee, WI 53203
(414) 297-3941
FAX (414) 297-4267

Wyoming:

100 East B Street, Room 4001
Casper, WY 82601
(307) 261-5761
FAX (307) 261-5499

Chapter 16:
Be A Pro—
Auction Insider Secrets

> "I was really impressed with the quality of cars being sold at a recent GSA auction I attended! I went to Edwards Air Force Base's fleet vehicle sale. The vehicles are regularly maintained and when you pay for the car you get a copy of its maintenance information. There is no sales tax — only a DMV registration fee."
>
> E. Stewart

Every auction has people who walk away with great bargains, and you're definitely going to be one of them. The one key is that the winners in this game follow a set of guidelines which the losers fail to recognize. In this chapter we will share the hard and fast rules with you, which will insure your entry into the "winner's circle"!

Before we get started discussing strategies, you may want to start becoming familiar with some of the basic terms which you will run across. These will apply, regardless of whether you are attending a public auction, submitting a sealed bid, spot bid, or even at most negotiated sales. You will want to make sure you understand these terms and conditions before you start bidding at auction.

Our **Glossary of Terms** begins on page 179 and gives you a summary of many commonly used terms. Take a few minutes now to read it and begin familiarizing yourself with some of the auction language you will be seeing on the auction notices. You'll feel much more at home. We did!

The following section also includes information on many publications which can assist you in making wise decisions before buying merchandise. The books and publications listed are some of the best available. Hopefully, you will be able to locate these in your local public library! If, however, you are seeking information and cannot find it locally, you may wish to contact the names and numbers we have provided to obtain your own copy.

Preparation

Your best strategy for successful auction shopping is to be prepared. The auctioneer has hundreds of hours of experience selling items at auction. While your bidding time may take only a few minutes, these few minutes may mean the difference between success and failure. You don't ever want to bid too high or drop out prematurely!

Perhaps the most important step initially is for you to determine exactly what it is you hope to buy at auction. Many people drift into an auction with no idea of what they intend to purchase. This is a big mistake for a number of reasons. Once of the most obvious being that you can get caught up in the frenzy and excitement of bidding and purchase something you either don't need — or worse — something that you can't easily resell.

So exactly what is it you wish to buy? Maybe it's a car. A computer. Antique furniture. Regardless of your interests, here are some simple steps you should follow which will help to assure you of a successful bid.

As we discussed earlier, most auction houses and governmental agencies have mailing lists for upcoming sales. You will want to contact as many of these as possible, so that you will be aware of any auctions you may wish to attend. When you receive a flier or notice, take a look at what is being offered. You may receive notices that are of no interest to you. On the other hand, you will probably see items of interest just about every time you get a flyer!

If you see something that interests you, give the auctioneer or government agency contact a phone call to make sure that the item will still be available at the auction. Once you have determined that a desired item will be at the auction, you will want to do the following so you can decide what the highest price you are willing to pay is:

- Locate a dealer or wholesaler in your area and find out what a similar item costs.

- Take a trip to the largest newsstand or bookstore in your area. See if you can locate books and magazines dealing with the item you desire. There are price books for computers, antiques, cars, boats, planes, etc. You may even find publications which list both wholesale and retail value.

- Stop by your local library and look for reference books that contain price lists.

- Check your local yellow pages for a company that handles repossessions or liquidations. Ask them how much similar items are selling for.

Almost any item you can buy at the mall will be available at auction. Would you be surprised to learn that many of the items you purchased brand new at retail prices were sold at auction before they reached your home? Wouldn't it be nice to cut out the middleman and purchase items at or below wholesale?

Here are some guidelines we have found useful. Regardless of whether you want to make a career of buying at auctions, add a little spare change to the kitty every month, or simply have an entertaining way to spend a Sunday afternoon shopping for bargains, these tidbits should be of great value to you.

Particular Purchase Strategies

Automobiles, Trucks, Vans & Pick-Ups

One of the most frequently used buying guides (and one with which you are probably already familiar) is the Blue Book. The Blue Book, which is just one edition of the National Automobile Dealer Association (N.A.D.A) Used Car Guides, provides price ranges for used automobiles.

While you are most likely aware of the Blue Book, have you ever heard of or seen the Yellow Book? This is another of their publications which gives the quotes on prices at dealerships across the country. The Blue Book does the same survey, but lists wholesale prices based on car auctions instead. In other words, the dealers look to the car auctions to set their prices on used cars.

These N.A.D.A. books are put to use by used car dealers, new car dealers (to determine trade-in values), financial institutions (as a guideline on what they will loan you to finance a car) and wholesalers (who purchase fleets for resale).

You can obtain an annual subscription, which would be wise for someone actively pursuing a career in reselling vehicles purchased at auction. If you are simply looking for one good buy you should be able to pick a single issue at a bookstore, or in your library. If you would like more information you can call:

**National Automobile Dealers
Used Car Guide Co.**
8400 Westpark Drive
Mc Lean, VA 22102
(703) 821-7193
(800) 544-6232
(800) 966-6232

The current rates and publications are as follows:

N.A.D.A. Used Car Guide:
This lists vehicles from 1987–1993.
$47.00/one-year subscription

N.A.D.A. Wholesale Used Car Trade-In Guide:
Lists 7 years of wholesale values.
$49.00/one-year subscription

N.A.D.A. Commercial Truck Guide:
Lists 10 years of used values.
$90.00/one-year subscription

N.A.D.A. Older Used Car Guide:
Lists 10 years of used value from 1977–1986
$50.00/one-year subscription

N.A.D.A. Title & Registration Book:
Summarizes Motor Vehicle laws, fees, and regulations.
$40.00/one-year subscription

N.A.D.A. Recreation Vehicle Appraisal Guide:
With 21 years of used values from 1973–1993, including 1994 suggested list prices.
$95.00/one-year subscription

N.A.D.A. Van Conversion/Limousine Appraisal Guide:
17 years of used values from 1977–1993, including 1994 suggested list prices.
$35.00/one-year subscription

N.A.D.A. Motorcycle/Snowmobile/ATV/Personal Watercraft Appraisal Guide:

18 years of used values from 1976–1992, including 1994 suggested list prices.
$45.00/one-year subscription

N.A.D.A. Small Boat Appraisal Guide:
18 years of used values from 1976–1993 for boats 7–25 feet, including 1994 suggested list prices.
$95.00/one-year subscription

N.A.D.A. Large Boat Appraisal Guide:
34 years of used values from 1960–1993 for boats 26 to 100 feet.
$65.00/one-year subscription

N.A.D.A. Retail Aircraft Appraisal Guide:
49 years of used values from 1945–1993.
$85.00/one-year subscription

N.A.D.A. Manufactured Housing Appraisal Guide:
40 years of used values from 1955–1994.
$95.00/one-year subscription

Please note that the subscription prices to these books are subject to change.

The **MacLean Hunter Market Reports** is another authority on automobile price lists. Their publication is known as the **Automobile Red Book.** To receive more detailed information about the publications they provide, you can contact:

> **MacLean Hunter Market Reports, Inc.**
> 29 N. Wacker Drive
> Chicago, IL 60606
> (312) 726-2802
> (312) 726-2574 (FAX)

MacLean Hunter has been in business since 1911 providing market reports on various and sundry subjects. The **Red Book** is published 8 times a year: (Jan. 1, Feb. 15, April 1, May 15, July 1, Aug. 15, Oct. 1, and Nov. 15). A subscription to the Red Book costs $49.50 per year.

They also have an **Older Car Red Book** which is published 4 times annually: (Jan. 1, April 1, July 1, and Oct. 1). A one-year subscription costs $69.00. Additionally, they publish a Truck Blue Book which comes out 4 times a year and costs $120.00. They also have subscriptions available for older trucks, commercial trailers, van conversions, mobile homes, recreational vehicles, boats and motorcycles.

For those of you with a computer, they even offer a custom electronic data base on all of their publications.

Dealers usually have their mechanics go to the pre-auction vehicle inspections. This would be a good idea for you, too! If you have a trusted mechanic you currently deal with, ask him or her if they would accompany you to inspect any vehicle you are thinking about buying. If you have to pay them to do this, think of it as money well spent. It could save you thousands!

Sometimes it's not very easy to do a really good inspection at some government auctions. While most will allow you to start the car up, most won't allow you to test drive. Some police auctions won't even allow you to open the car prior to purchase — you even have to hire a locksmith to make you a key. Remember — these have been confiscated! For the most part, confiscated automobiles should be in pretty good shape — they were probably up and running when they were taken.

The following is a basic checklist which should help you to decide whether or not you want to make an offer on a vehicle, and if so, how much you should bid.

The Outside

The first thing you should look at is the appearance of the car:

1. How does the paint job look? This will tell you a lot about not only the condition of the vehicle in question, but also the person(s) who owned it previously. A shoddy, sloppy paint job should warn you of a cheap, quick repair of something more serious. If you see paint on the chrome or around moldings, if the inside and outside are two different colors, or if you can see air bubbles or brush marks—this can spell trouble. A new paint job on a vehicle may be hiding rust or damage.

Check for bondo, too. This is a type of filler used on car bodies when they have dents and rust problems that can't be pounded out or repaired. TIP: Whenever you're inspecting used cars, carry a magnet with you. If you run the magnet along the body of the car (making sure you aren't damaging paint!!) you will be able to tell if you're looking at metal or a filler. If you don't have a magnet available, you can gently knock on the sides of the car. If you don't hear a hollow sound, you're probably not knocking on metal!

2. Make sure you roll up your sleeves and get down on the ground to look under the car. If you see areas of heavy rust, holes, a broken tail pipe, puddles, etc., you may be looking at potential problems. It's not a bad idea to bring a small flashlight with you so you can really see under the car.

Identifying the cause of a puddle of fluid under a vehicle may save you serious trouble down the road. Small stains or an occasional drop are probably nothing to be too concerned about. But wet spots deserve attention and bigger puddles should be of real concern.

Fluids can be identified by their color and consistency:

• Yellowish green, pastel blue or fluorescent orange colors indicate an overheated engine or an antifreeze leak caused by a bad hose, water pump, or leaking radiator.

• Dark brown or black oily fluid means the engine is leaking oil. The leak could be caused by a bad seal or gasket.

• A red oily spot indicates a transmission or power steering fluid leak. Both of these can be costly repairs.

• A puddle of clear water is generally not a problem. It may be normal condensation from the vehicle's air conditioning system.

If you are able to start the vehicle up during the inspection — listen to your nose! Some problems can be detected simply by doing a bit of sniffing. You might want to consider the following problems if you smell something funny:

• If you smell a light, sharp odor sort of like burnt toast this can signal an electrical short or burning insulation. Have your mechanic take a good look!

• If you smell something like rotten eggs or a harsh sulfur smell this usually indicates a problem with the catalytic converter or other emission control devices. This is also something for your mechanic to observe.

• If you smell a thick, acrid odor, it usually means oil is burning. Not a good sign! Look for a leak.

• If you smell gasoline vapors after you try to start the car and have failed, you may just have flooded the engine. Wait a few minutes and try again. If you constantly smell gas, you may have a leak in the fuel system. This is a potentially dangerous problem that will need immediate repair.

• If you smell something like burning resin or chemical odors, it may signal an overheated clutch or brakes. Check the parking brake. Note: This will only occur if you are actually able to drive the vehicle.

• A sweet, steamy odor tells you there is a coolant leak.

3. The tailpipe can tell you about some real problems, even if you can't start the car up! Rub your finger on the inside of the tailpipe. If you get black and gummy slime on your hands, the car may need a ring or valve job. If it's merely black and sooty, the car probably only needs a tune up. The difference in the cost of repairs is of major significance! TIP: A word to the wise (and clean). Keep a few "wet wipes" on hand, and something you can clean your hands on, so that you can check from car to car without confusing yourself as to which one was oily, sooty, etc. Otherwise, after a few cars, you won't know which one was which. You may also wish to take along a pocket notebook to write down your observations on the cars you plan to bid on. This will come in handy when the bidding begins.

4. When you push on the car to make it bounce, it should only bounce one time after you stop. More than this means the car needs new shocks. While putting new shocks on a car isn't too expensive, damage can be done to a car that is driven too long without good shocks!

5. While you don't need to kick the tires, you certainly should take a look at them. Are they worn in a uniform manner? Uneven tread can mean that the car is out of alignment. More seriously, it can mean that the car has been in an accident and there are problems with the axles or tie rods. If you see an old clunker with new tires, it can mean all you're going to get out of that deal is new tires!

6. Squeaks, squeals, rattles, rumbles and other sounds can give you valuable clues about problems and maintenance needs. Here are some common noises and what they may indicate:

• SQUEAL—A shrill, sharp noise, usually related to engine speed (again, you will have to be able to start the car to observe this). This noise can mean you have loose or worn power steering, fan or air conditioning belts.

• CLICK—A slight, sharp noise, related to either engine speed or vehicle speed can mean you have a loose wheel cover, loose or bent fan blade, a stuck valve lifter or low engine oil.

• SCREECH—A high-pitched, piercing metallic sound, usually occurs while the vehicle is in motion and indicates brake wear.

• RUMBLE—A low-pitched, rhythmic sound can tell you a car has a defective exhaust pipe, converter or muffler, a worn universal joint or other drive-line component.

• PING—A high-pitched metallic tapping sound which occurs when when the car is running fast is usually caused by fuel with a lower octane rating than recommended.

• HEAVY KNOCK—A rhythmic pounding sound can mean that you have a worn crankshaft or connecting rod bearings—or a loose transmission torque converter.

• CLUNK—A random thumping sound can mean you have loose shock absorbers or other suspension components. It can also mean a loose exhaust pipe or muffler.

7. TRUST YOUR FEELINGS! Difficult handling, a rough ride, vibration and poor performance are the kinds of symptoms you can feel. Again, these will be hard to determine if you are only allowed to start the engine at an auction preview. Here are a few guidelines for those of you who are able to actually test drive:

• STEERING—Wandering or having difficulty steering in a straight linecan be caused by misaligned front wheels and/or worn steering components, which can include the idler arm or ball joints.

• PULLING—If the vehicle has a tendency to pull to the right or the left, this can be caused by something as simple as under-inflated tires or something as serious as a damaged or mis-aligned front end.

The Inside:

Now let's move to the interior of the car:

1. Take a look at the odometer. It is against the law for anyone to set back an odometer. If you see a car with an unrealistic odometer reading, a simple rule of thumb is to multiply the age of the car by 12,000. If the car is three years old, you can expect the odometer reading to be in the ballpark of 36,000 miles. Granted, when you are buying surplus automobiles from a government agency, the readings may be higher than this because the car may have been used more than a family car would be. What you really want to be looking for are cars that appear to have much more wear and tear than the odometer is indicating.

2. When you open the passenger side door, how does it feel? Does it open well, or does it squeak? Does the door drop and fall? A weak driver's door can mean the person who owned the car didn't treat it very well.

3. Be sure to look under the car mats and push on the floor panels. Check for rust at the bottom of the door frame. Look under the dashboard for loose or hanging wires. Pushing on the roof areas will give you a better feel for the car's real condition — and will affect the resale value of the car.

4. Look inside the radiator. If the water is rusty, the radiator may need to be replaced. If there is engine oil leaking in the cooling system and you see a shiny, oily film, this indicates there are going to be expensive repairs involved.

5. Check the dipstick. If the oil is gummy and gritty, the car has been poorly maintained. A milky brown or gray oil indicates expensive repairs in the forecast. See how thick the oil is. Sometimes heavier weight oils are used to hide valve lifter noises or other engine problems.

If you are able to start the car up — or have someone else start it, pay close attention. Stand behind the car when it is being started. Does it start easily? What kind of smoke comes out of the exhaust? (Blue smoke means serious engine problems!) Look under the hood after it's started. Is it shaking badly? If so, you may need new motor mounts. Have someone run it through the gears. If you hear clunking you probably have transmission problems.

Vehicles are usually the second most expensive purchase we make after buying a home. When you are making a bid, keep the cost of potential repairs planted firmly in your mind.

Computers

Computers are becoming more and more plentiful at auctions, in part because the systems are enhanced and upgraded so quickly, thereby producing instant obsolescence! This leaves the field wide open for individuals wishing to capitalize on low prices. An auction may be a great place for you to find a bargain priced personal computer. If you are entertaining the idea of buying for resale, you will want to proceed carefully.

Information on computers abounds. Unfortunately, the vast majority of today's information might as well be written in a foreign language unless you happen to be a real computer buff. If you don't know your bytes from a hole in the ground, you will want to read as much as you can on the various types of systems available and exactly what their capabilities are.

Price lists are readily available in many computer magazines. You can expect retail prices to be about double what you would pay whole-sale.

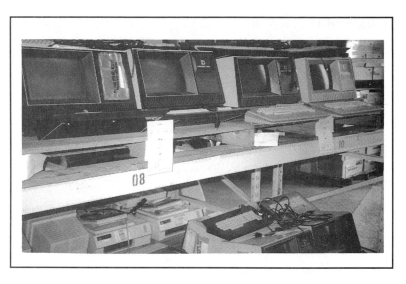

Just as car professionals rely on N.A.D.A and MacLean Hunter, the computer trade looks to the **COMPUTER HOT LINE** for information on products and prices. You can subscribe on a weekly or monthly basis, depending upon your needs, and a monthly subscription can run as little as $31 a year if you have it sent to you via Third Class mail.

They also publish a monthly newsletter for buying and selling tele-communications equipment. This is called **TELECOM GEAR** and is avail-able for $31 a year again via Third Class mail.

Another place to look for guidelines on what to pay for computers, audio and video equipment, cameras, car stereos, guitars, televisions, etc. is Orion Research Corporation. Orion specializes in putting out the Orion Blue Books. Here's a brief overview of what they have to offer. The address and telephone number of the Orion Research Corporation have been pro-vided for you at the end of this listing.

Computers:
Over 26,987 hardware products from over 1000 manufacturers. Lists prices on systems, fax machines, monitors, printers, plotters, scanners, modems, disk drives, tape backups, terminals, etc.

Audio:
Over 48,086 products from over 1400 manufacturers. Lists current prices for cassettes, 4 and 8 track tape cartridges, CD players, digital audio tape play-ers, equalizers, integrated and power amplifiers, preamplifiers, speakers, receivers, reel-to-reels, signal processors, systems, turntables, and more.

Video and Television:

Over 21,835 products from over 450 manufacturers. Price lists include: TV's, VCR's, camcorders, laser videodisc players, black & white cameras, color video cameras, broadcast cameras, electronic still video cameras, lenses, professional recorder/players, remote controls, and more.

Cameras:

Includes over 17,165 products from 400 manufacturers. Lists the following: 35mm cameras, medium format, press view, Instamatic, disc, SLR and self-professing cameras, lenses, tack, bellows, viewfinders, enlargers, exposure meters, slide projectors and viewers, movie cameras and projectors, etc.

Car Stereos:

Over 21,333 products from over 200 manufacturers are listed: cassette receivers, CD players, digital audio tape players, equalizers, power amps, mobile CB units, scanners, walkie-talkies, speakers, radar detectors, etc.

Guitars & Musical Instruments:

Over 38,048 products from over 450 manufacturers, this lists price ranges for the following: guitars, guitar amps, tuners, drums, cymbals, banjos, brass winds, wood winds, cellos, harps, dulcimers, keyboards, keyboard amps, mandolins, marimbas, synthesizers, violins, xylophones, etc.

Vintage Guitars:

Over 7,358 vintage guitars are listed. This publication comes out four times a year.

Professional Sound:

Over 24,281 products from over 350 manufacturers. Lists the following: monitors, microphones, equalizers, enclosures, mixing boards, reel-to-reels, signal processors, wireless systems, crossover networks, integrated and power amplifiers, raw speaker components, PA systems.

Copiers:

Over 1,858 copiers and typewriters listed. If you look at the Notice of Award we show on pg. 195, you will see that one lucky bidder purchased 8 IBM electric typewriters at auction for only $105—quite a bargain! These were all IBM Selectrics.

Guns:
Over 8,678 products from over 300 manufacturers. Lists values on handguns, rifles, shotguns and black powder firearms.

Tools:
Over 8,733 products from over 120 manufacturers are listed. Lists include prices for compressors, pumps, generators, saws, power screwdrivers, demolition tools, planers, chisels, scalers, boring drills, nailers, and more.

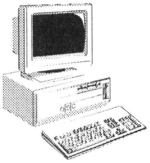

Video Equivalency Chart:
Lists over 8,175 products from over 200 manufacturers. This book lists equivalent machines from different manufacturers, and includes VCRs and camcorders.

How to Buy and Price a Used Computer:
"Everything you have always wanted to know about used computers, but didn't know where to look." This book lists over 22,750 computer hardware products as well as the major software packages available, used equipment dealers, and an overview answering basic questions about computers.

As you can see, for someone seriously interested in buying used items at auction for resale, Orion has a highly valuable selection of books from which to choose. If you would like more information on any of their products, contact them at the following address:

ORION RESEARCH CORPORATION
14555 N. Scottsdale Road #330
Scottsdale, AZ 85254
(602) 951-1114

Antiques and Collectibles

Many of you will find that you enjoy attending auctions which feature antiques and collectible items. For the most part, estate sales will provide you with the sorts of things you are seeking. Public auctions generally have some antiques and collectibles. Additionally, there are auctions which specialize in just this type of merchandise. You may find a U.S. Marshals Service auction which features the more exotic items, since businessmen and outlaws are often fond of collecting. <u>Many</u> private auction houses specialize in antiques. Check your Volume 2 listing, as well as your local newspaper, for information on upcoming auctions you may wish to attend.

Your library should have books which deal with appraising antiques and collectibles. A couple of titles you should be looking for include: <u>Kovel's Antique and Collectible Price List</u> and <u>Schroeder's Antique Price Guide.</u> Both of these books are published annually and provide excellent information on appraiser-approved prices. As an example, Schroeder's current guide gives price information on approximately 50,000 items in almost 500 categories. As you can see, this type of pricing guide can be invaluable.

The following notice for an Estate Auction features many antiques and collectibles. You will notice the extensive number of items being offered at auction. Due to the large amount of available items, the auction was held over a two-day period. See how this auction notice shows the terms of the auction. I'm sure by now you are becoming more familiar with what many of the terms mean! (See also Glossary pages 179-190)

COUNTY OF SANTA BARBARA PUBLIC ADMINISTRATOR-GUARDIAN
SPECTACULAR TWO DAY

ESTATE AUCTION

Saturday, November 19 and Sunday, November 20   10:00 a.m. each day
Preview from 8:30 until sale time each day.

Auctioneer's Note: This auction will consist of the exceptionally fine antiques and collectibles from a Hope Ranch estate and from other estates in Santa Barbara County. The sale will last two days to accommodate the great number of items to be auctioned. The public is invited to attend these major auctions.

SATURDAY

This auction includes a pair of hand painted etageres w/hand painted floral decor and Queen Anne legs, pair of white chairs w/needlepoint seats, spinet piano and bench, paintings signed: Jules Dahlager, mahogany bow-front chest-on-chest, several small old hand crafted rugs, many boxes of fine bric-a-brac, Edison concert cylindrical phonograph, Cress electric kilns, cobalt blue dishes/glasses, Wedgewood and Noritake luncheon sets, Belleek tea pot w/sugar and creamer, boxes of miniatures, lovely old framed prints, chocolate set, set of china by Pickard and a 155 piece set of Peruvian sterling, old cameras, saddles, rocker w/needlepoint seat, various sterling silver items, jewelry items including ladies platinum ring w/diamonds, old clocks, cut crystal, figurines, Limoges plates, contemporary furniture, Honda "Elite" scooter and so much more. Please come early and see it all.

SUNDAY

The Sunday auction will include: Old castor sets, ladies slant front desk, matching chairs w/needlepoint seats, mandolin and case, pair of matched cloisonne ginger jars, pr. of drop-leaf tables, stereoptic viewer and cards, many lots of fine linens, tilt-top candle stand, video camera, old dollsby Nora Welling, Cuno & Otto Dressel and others, wicker furniture, cast iron bank, boxes of old metal soldiers, circus etc., 26 pieces of Fostoria stemware, 78 piece set of Limoges Haviland china, Singer Featherweight sewing machines, autoharp, Victorian marble top parlor table, three drawer chest w/acorn and oak leaf motif, many boxes of high quality bric-a-brac, Mah Jong sets, spectacular old clocks, collector coins and currency, sets of sterling flatware, jewelry and gold pocket watches/some with diamonds, Packard Bell and other computers, Shirley Temple milk pitchers and hundreds of lots of commensurate quality. Come early and see.

TERMS: Cash or checks (On our approval), to be paid in full at each auction. Check-out following each auction. All items are sold AS-IS, WHERE-IS, without warranty expressed or implied. All representations of the merchandise are believed to be correct, however, the buyer must depend solely on his/her own judgment as to the value, if any, of the merchandise. Some items may be removed from the sale prior to the sale at the discretion of the Public Administrator/Guardian.

Public Administrator/Guardian
County of Santa Barbara

State Bond Number 146637300136

Art, Jewelry and Coins

Art has sold at auction for hundreds of years. While most of us have seen movies depicting an art auction at Sotheby's or Christie's, not too many of us would actually know how to place value on fine art. Never fear, there is a publication which can help you become much better versed in this area.

Knowledgeable collectors subscribe to Art & Auction magazine. The magazine is published monthly and has a special edition once a year which provides an International directory. You might want to see if your local library carries this magazine so you can take a look to see if it deals with the type of information of interest to you.

Below we show a few items from auction flyers we received. This gives you an idea of the fine quality of merchandise you can expect to find at auctions.

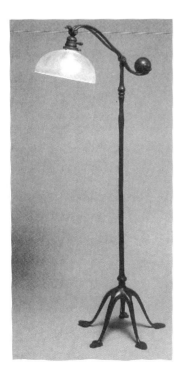

Chapter 17:
More Government Programs

> "I purchase mostly computers and laser printers. I think the RTC and FDIC auctions are the best. FDIC equipment is well-maintained and up to date. I bought a whole load (15 units) of computers for $200, and was able to sell them for $75 each in L.A. If you're cautious you'll make money."
>
> A. Morey

W hile putting this book together, we researched and read about many, many existing programs which can provide you with opportunities to buy at auction. Here is an overview of some of the more popular programs with information on how to get involved.

Tennessee Valley Authority

The Tennessee Valley Authority (TVA) is involved in a variety of activities ranging from flood control and electric power production to forestry and wildlife development. The TVA sells both personal and real property, such as electrical supplies, computers, heavy construction equipment, office furniture and machines, vehicles ranging from heavy industrial vehicles to pick-up trucks and sedans, and undeveloped land for industrial and recreational purposes. Over 50 sales are held by the TVA each year throughout Tennessee, Alabama, Kentucky, Mississippi and North Carolina.

Goods are first offered to current employees and retirees at a set price. The items remaining are sold through auction. Sales information is advertised through mailing lists, newspapers and trade publications. To be placed on TVA mailing lists, write to the address on the following page. Make sure you include the types of items you are interested in so you will be placed on the appropriate mailing list.

Personal checks up to $25,000 are accepted; company checks are accepted up to $50,000. Amounts higher than $50,000 require a certified or cashier's check. For information, write or call:

Tennessee Valley Authority
Transportation and Surplus Sales
605 Chestnut Street
P.O. Box 11127
Chattanooga, TN 37401-2127
(615) 751-2635

Department of the Treasury
Bureau of Alcohol, Tobacco, and Firearms

The Bureau of Alcohol, Tobacco and Firearms sells a limited number of Bureau owned motor vehicles and seized vehicles. Vehicles range from sports cars to family sedans and are disposed of in an "as is" condition. The vast majority of these vehicles are reported by the Bureau to the Federal Supply Service of the General Services Administration for disposal. The GSA decides if the cars are economical or practical for the General Services Administration to sell. If the GSA does not take the cars, it authorizes the Bureau to dispose of them.

Sales are advertised in local newspapers. Agency personnel also contact salvage and scrap firms to obtain bids for badly damaged vehicles. The Bureau of Alcohol, Tobacco and Firearms accepts only cashier's checks or postal money orders. No cash is accepted. If you would like more information, contact:

Bureau of Alcohol, Tobacco, and Firearms
Administrative Programs Division
Facilities Management Branch
650 Massachusetts Avenue, NW
Washington, DC 20226

Department of the Interior/Bureau of Land Management

The Bureau of Land Management (BLM) is responsible for the management of more than 270 million acres of public lands. The land, which is located primarily in the West and in Alaska, is sold to the public under certain conditions. The unimproved or undeveloped land is generally rural wooded, grassland, or desert. The land is sold through direct sale and competitive sales such as auctions. Sales are listed in the Federal Register, which you can probably find at your local library.

The BLM can sell public land only to U.S. citizens or corporations subject to Federal or state laws. No financing is available. Cashier's check or cash is required. For more information, contact the following:

Alabama:
Bureau of Land Management
Eastern States Office
7450 Boston Blvd.
Springfield, VA 22153

Colorado:
Bureau of Land Management
2850 Youngfield Street
Lakewood, CO 80215-7076

Alaska:
Bureau of Land Management
222 W. 7th Avenue, #13 Street
Anchorage, AK 99513-7599

Connecticut:
Bureau of Land Management
Eastern States Office
7450 Boston Blvd.
Springfield, VA 22153

Arizona:
Bureau of Land Management
3707 North 7th Street
Phoenix, AZ 85011

Delaware:
Bureau of Land Management
Eastern States Office
7450 Boston Blvd.
Springfield, VA 22153

Arkansas:
Bureau of Land Management
Eastern States Office
7450 Boston Blvd.
Springfield, VA 22153

District of Columbia:
Bureau of Land Management
Eastern States Office
7450 Boston Blvd.
Springfield, VA 22153

California:
Bureau of Land Management
2800 Cottage Way, E-2841
Sacramento, CA 95825

Florida:
Bureau of Land Management
Eastern States Office
7450 Boston Blvd.
Springfield, VA 22153

Georgia:
Bureau of Land Management
Eastern States Office
7450 Boston Blvd.
Springfield, VA 22153

Idaho:
Bureau of Land Management
3380 Americana Terrace
Boise, ID 83706

Illinois:
Bureau of Land Management
Eastern States Office
7450 Boston Blvd.
Springfield, VA 22153

Indiana:
Bureau of Land Management
Eastern States Office
7450 Boston Blvd.
Springfield, VA 22153

Iowa:
Bureau of Land Management
Eastern States Office
7450 Boston Blvd.
Springfield, VA 22153

Kansas:
Bureau of Land Management
1474 Rodeo Road
P.O. Box 27115
Santa Fe, NM 87505-7115

Kentucky:
Bureau of Land Management
Eastern States Office
7450 Boston Blvd.
Springfield, VA 22153

Louisiana:
Bureau of Land Management
Eastern States Office
7450 Boston Blvd.
Springfield, VA 22153

Maine:
Bureau of Land Management
Eastern States Office
7450 Boston Blvd.
Springfield, VA 22153

Maryland:
Bureau of Land Management
Eastern States Office
7450 Boston Blvd.
Springfield, VA 22153

Massachusetts:
Bureau of Land Management
Eastern States Office
7450 Boston Blvd.
Springfield, VA 22153

Michigan:
Bureau of Land Management
Eastern States Office
7450 Boston Blvd.
Springfield, VA 22153

Minnesota:
Bureau of Land Management
Eastern States Office
7450 Boston Blvd.
Springfield, VA 22153

Mississippi:
Bureau of Land Management
Eastern States Office
7450 Boston Blvd.
Springfield, VA 22153

Missouri:
Bureau of Land Management
Eastern States Office
7450 Boston Blvd.
Springfield, VA 22153

Montana:
Bureau of Land Management
222 N. 32nd Street
P.O. Box 36800
Billings, MT 59107

Nebraska:
Bureau of Land Management
2515 Warren Avenue
P.O. Box 1828
Cheyenne, WY 82003

Nevada:
Bureau of Land Management
850 Harvard Way
P.O. Box 12000
Reno, NV 89520-0006

New Hampshire:
Bureau of Land Management
Eastern States Office
7450 Boston Blvd.
Springfield, VA 22153

New Jersey:
Bureau of Land Management
Eastern States Office
7450 Boston Blvd.
Springfield, VA 22153

New Mexico:
Bureau of Land Management
P.O. Box 27115
1474 Rodeo Road
Santa Fe, NM 87505-7115

New York:
Bureau of Land Management
Eastern States Office
7450 Boston Blvd.
Springfield, VA 22153

North Carolina:
Bureau of Land Management
Eastern States Office
7450 Boston Blvd.
Springfield, VA 22153

North Dakota:
Bureau of Land Management
222 N. 32nd Street
P.O. Box 36800
Billings, MT 59107

Ohio:
Bureau of Land Management
Eastern States Office
7450 Boston Blvd.
Springfield, VA 22153

Oklahoma:
Bureau of Land Management
1474 Rodeo Road
P.O. Box 27115
Santa Fe, NM 87505-7115

Oregon:
Bureau of Land Management
1300 NE 44th Avenue
P.O. Box 2965
Portland, OR 97208

Pennsylvania:
Bureau of Land Management
Eastern States Office
7450 Boston Blvd.
Springfield, VA 22153

Rhode Island:
Bureau of Land Management
Eastern States Office
7450 Boston Blvd.
Springfield, VA 22153

South Carolina:
Bureau of Land Management
Eastern States Office
7450 Boston Blvd.
Springfield, VA 22153

South Dakota:
Bureau of Land Management
222 N. 32nd Street
P.O. Box 36800
Billings, MT 59107

Tennessee:
Bureau of Land Management
Eastern States Office
7450 Boston Blvd.
Springfield, VA 22153

Texas:
Bureau of Land Management
1474 Rodeo Road
P.O. Box 27115
Santa Fe, NM 87505-7115

Utah:
CFS Financial Center—301
324 South State Street
Salt Lake City, UT 84111-2303

Vermont:
Bureau of Land Management
Eastern States Office
7450 Boston Blvd.
Springfield, VA 22153

Virginia:
Bureau of Land Management
Eastern States Office
7450 Boston Blvd.
Springfield, VA 22153

Washington:
Bureau of Land Management
1300 NE 44th Avenue
P.O. Box 2965
Portland, OR 97208

West Virginia:
Bureau of Land Management
Eastern States Office
7450 Boston Blvd.
Springfield, VA 22153

Wisconsin:
Bureau of Land Management
Eastern States Office
7450 Boston Blvd.
Springfield, VA 22153

Wyoming:
Bureau of Land Management
2515 Warren Avenue
P.O. Box 1828
Cheyenne, WY 82003

Federal Deposit Insurance Corporation

The Federal Deposit Insurance Corporation (FDIC) sells a wide range of assets from failed banks including loans, real estate such as undeveloped land,  hotels, shopping malls, single-family homes, condominiums, and apartment complexes. They also sell personal property including computers, phone systems, furniture and fixtures, plants, and specialty items like crystal, china and antiques.

The FDIC advertises their sales in the Wall Street Journal and local newspapers. They also have the broadcast media inform their listeners about when sales are scheduled. The regional FDIC offices listed here can also provide information on upcoming sales in your area. The FDIC does not maintain a national mailing list.

If you would like more information, contact **FDIC, Asset Marketing,** at the FDIC regional office where you are interested in buying property, or call and ask for Asset Marketing, Customer Service:

Alabama:
FDIC
Asset Marketing
500 W. Monroe, Suite 3200
Chicago, IL 60661
(312) 382-6000

Alaska:
FDIC
Asset Marketing
25 Ecker Street, Suite 1900
San Francisco, CA 94105
(415) 546-1810

Arizona:
FDIC
Asset Martketing
25 Ecker Street, Suite 1900
San Francisco, CA 94105
(415) 546-1810

Arkansas:
FDIC
Asset Marketing
500 W. Monroe, Suite 3200
Chicago, IL 60661
(312) 382-6000

California:
FDIC
Asset Marketing
25 Ecker Street, Suite 1900
San Francisco, CA 94105
(415) 546-1810

Colorado:
FDIC
Asset Marketing
25 Ecker Street, Suite 1900
San Francisco, CA 94105
(415) 546-1810

Connecticut:
FDIC
Asset Marketing
452 5th Avenue, 21st Floor
New York, NY 10018
(212) 704-1200

Delaware:
FDIC
Asset Marketing
500 W. Monroe, Suite 3200
Chicago, IL 60661
(312) 382-6000

District of Columbia:
FDIC
Asset Marketing
500 W. Monroe, Suite 3200
Chicago, IL 60661
(312) 382-6000

Florida:
FDIC
Asset Marketing
500 W. Monroe, Suite 3200
Chicago, IL 60661
(312) 382-6000

Georgia:
FDIC
Asset Marketing
500 W. Monroe, Suite 3200
Chicago, IL 60661
(312) 382-6000

Hawaii:
FDIC
Asset Marketing
25 Ecker Street, Suite 1900
San Francisco, CA 94105
(415) 546-1810

Idaho:
FDIC
Asset Marketing
25 Ecker Street, Suite 1900
San Francisco, CA 94105
(415) 546-1810

Illinois:
FDIC
Asset Marketing
500 W. Monroe, Suite 3200
Chicago, IL 60661
(312) 382-6000

Indiana:
FDIC
Asset Marketing
500 W. Monroe, Suite 3200
Chicago, IL 60661
(312) 382-6000

Iowa:
FDIC
Asset Marketing
500 W. Monroe, Suite 3200
Chicago, IL 60661
(312) 382-6000

Kansas:
FDIC
Asset Marketing
500 W. Monroe, Suite 3200
Chicago, IL 60661
(312) 382-6000

Kentucky:
FDIC
Asset Marketing
500 W. Monroe, Suite 3200
Chicago, IL 60661
(312) 382-6000

Louisiana:

FDIC
Asset Marketing
500 W. Monroe, Suite 3200
Chicago, IL 60661
(312) 382-6000

Maine:

FDIC
Asset Marketing
452 5th Avenue, 21st Floor
New York, NY 10018
(312) 207-0200

Maryland:

FDIC
Asset Marketing
500 W. Monroe, Suite 3200
Chicago, IL 60661
(312) 382-6000

Massachusetts:

FDIC
Asset Marketing
452 5th Avenue, 21st Floor
New York, NY 10018
(212) 704-1200

Michigan:

FDIC
Asset Marketing
500 W. Monroe, Suite 3200
Chicago, IL 60661
(312) 382-6000

Minnesota:

FDIC
Asset Marketing
500 W. Monroe, Suite 3200
Chicago, IL 60661
(312) 382-6000

Mississippi:

FDIC
Asset Marketing
500 W. Monroe, Suite 3200
Chicago, IL 60661
(312) 382-6000

Missouri:

FDIC
Asset Marketing
500 W. Monroe, Suite 3200
Chicago, IL 60661
(312) 382-6000

Montana:

FDIC
Asset Marketing
25 Ecker Street, Suite 1900
San Francisco, CA 94105
(415) 546-1810

Nebraska:

FDIC
Asset Marketing
500 W. Monroe, Suite 3200
Chicago, IL 60661
(312) 382-6000

New Hampshire:

FDIC
Asset Marketing
452 5th Avenue, 21st Floor
New York, NY 10018
(212) 704-1200

New Jersey:

FDIC
Asset Marketing
452 5th Avenue, 21st Floor
New York, NY 10018
(212) 704-1200

New Mexico:
FDIC
Asset Marketing
25 Ecker Street, Suite 1900
San Francisco, CA 94105
(415) 546-1810

New York:
FDIC
Asset Marketing
452 5th Avenue, 21st Floor
New York, NY 10018
(212) 704-1200

North Carolina:
FDIC
Asset Marketing
500 W. Monroe, Suite 3200
Chicago, IL 60661
(312) 382-6000

North Dakota:
FDIC
Asset Marketing
500 W. Monroe, Suite 3200
Chicago, IL 60661
(312) 382-6000

Ohio:
FDIC
Asset Marketing
500 W. Monroe, Suite 3200
Chicago, IL 60661
(312) 382-6000

Oklahoma:
FDIC
Asset Marketing
1910 Pacific Avenue, Suite 1700
Dallas, TX 75201
(214) 754-0098

Oregon:
FDIC
Asset Marketing
25 Ecker Street, Suite 1900
San Francisco, CA 94105
(415) 546-1810

Pennsylvania:
FDIC
Asset Marketing
452 5th Avenue, 21st Floor
New York, NY 10018
(212) 704-1200

Rhode Island:
FDIC
Asset Marketing
452 5th Avenue, 21st Floor
New York, NY 10018
(212) 704-1200

South Carolina:
FDIC
Asset Marketing
500 W. Monroe, Suite 3200
Chicago, IL 60661
(312) 382-6000

South Dakota:
FDIC
Asset Marketing
500 W. Monroe, Suite 3200
Chicago, IL 60661
(312) 382-6000

Tennessee:
FDIC
Asset Marketing
500 W. Monroe, Suite 3200
Chicago, IL 60661
(312) 382-6000

Texas:
FDIC
Asset Marketing
1910 Pacific Avenue, Suite 1700
Dallas, TX 75201

Utah:
FDIC
Asset Marketing
25 Ecker Street, Suite 1900
San Francisco, CA 94105
(415) 546-1810

Vermont:
FDIC
Asset Marketing
452 5th Avenue, 21st Floor
New York, NY 10018
(212) 704-1200

Virginia:
FDIC
Asset Marketing
500 W. Monroe, Suite 3200
Chicago, IL 60661
(312) 382-6000

Washington:
FDIC
Asset Marketing
25 Ecker Street, Suite 1900
San Francisco, CA 94105
(415) 546-1810

West Virginia:
FDIC
Asset Marketing
500 W. Monroe, Suite 3200
Chicago, IL 60661
(312) 382-6000

Wisconsin:
FDIC
Asset Marketing
500 W. Monroe, Suite 3200
Chicago, IL 60661
(312) 382-6000

Wyoming:
FDIC
Asset Marketing
25 Ecker Street, Suite 1900
San Francisco, CA 94105
(415) 546-1810

Department of Agriculture

The Department of Agriculture (USDA) sells trucks, ambulances, station wagons, sedans, office equipment, office furniture, computers, and laboratory items.

Although most cars are sent to the GSA for sale, a few vehicles are periodically sold at USDA's field offices around the country. Sedans and station wagons make up a large majority of the cars at these sales. The Farmer's Home Administration (FmHA) of the USDA sells real property such as foreclosed houses and farms to the public.

Personal property is sold through auction or sealed bid. The sales are advertised through notices in Federal Government buildings and newspapers. Your local real estate agent will also have listings. A mailing list is maintained for sales in the Washington, DC area only.

If you want more information on the USDA's sales, look in the phone book under the "U.S. Government" listings for the USDA office closest to you. Most likely, you state capital has a USDA office.

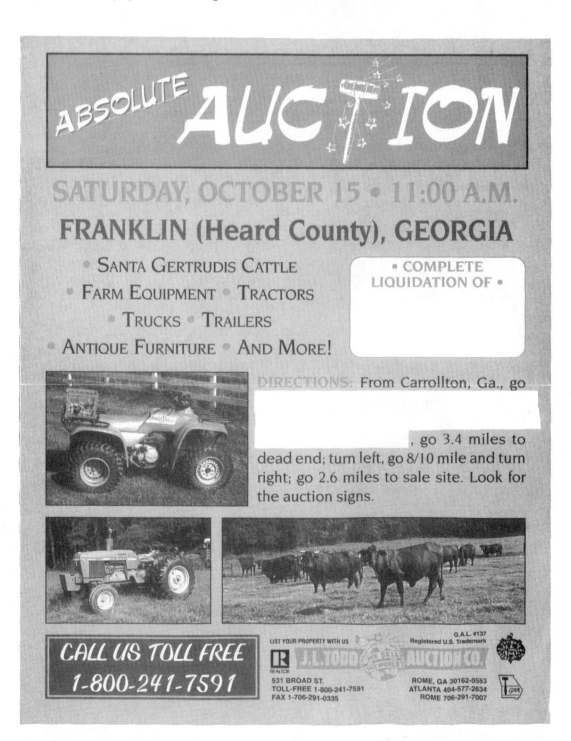

ABSOLUTE AUCTION

SATURDAY, OCTOBER 15 • 11:00 A.M.

FRANKLIN (Heard County), GEORGIA

- SANTA GERTRUDIS CATTLE
- FARM EQUIPMENT • TRACTORS
- TRUCKS • TRAILERS
- ANTIQUE FURNITURE • AND MORE!

• COMPLETE LIQUIDATION OF •

DIRECTIONS: From Carrollton, Ga., go ... , go 3.4 miles to dead end; turn left, go 8/10 mile and turn right; go 2.6 miles to sale site. Look for the auction signs.

CALL US TOLL FREE
1-800-241-7591

LIST YOUR PROPERTY WITH US   J.L. TODD   AUCTION CO.
G.A.L. #137
Registered U.S. Trademark
531 BROAD ST.
TOLL-FREE 1-800-241-7591
FAX 1-706-291-0335
ROME, GA 30162-0553
ATLANTA 404-577-2634
ROME 706-291-7007

Chapter 18:
Charity Auctions
&
Other Hidden Treasures

"Charity auctions are great places for real bargains because <u>everything has to be sold that day!</u> Many charities will employ professional auctioneers who make sure everything will sell, and sell for a fair price. If bidders have done their homework and know the value of what they're bidding on, they can often walk away with great deals!"

Mary James, Certified Auctioneers Institute

Charitable organizations have known for a long time that holding an auction is a great way to raise money. The items that go up for bid are almost always donated by individuals who want to help the non-profit group. So, the cost to the charity is absolutely nothing for the goods, and zero dollars for the volunteer staff to organize the auction. Their only expense is a modest fee for the auctioneer. For these reasons, many very good bargains can be found at countless charity auctions in every community throughout the US.

We've found that more and more charities are conducting auctions regularly. This means that in any average sized town or city, you can find a worthwhile charity auction at least once a month. Often the charity will hold an evening auction with a preview of the items scheduled a few hours before the actual bidding. In the case of some charities, however, items are displayed and sealed bids are taken. This is called a silent auction. Each charity, and each chapter of national charities have different policies — and some vary their methods of selling from year to year. Whatever the method the charity chooses, the good news for any prospective bidder is this: the competition for any given item will most likely be limited, as most charities don't advertise broadly, so the number of people attending can be rather low. Disappointing for the charity, but a field day for the bidder.

Following is an overview of various types of charity auctions and some specific organizations that have regular opportunities for the average person.

The Salvation Army — Cars! Cars! Cars!

This organization has thrift stores in nearly every community, but they also have a great number of Adult Rehabilitation Centers which typically receive donated automobiles. These cars come to that organization from individuals who don't want to bother with a used car lot, who want the tax write-off, and who want to help the Salvation Army.

The Salvation Army breaks down the USA into four regions: Western, Central, Eastern and Southern. The Eastern region sends all of its donated cars, including boats, to a Pittsburgh auto auction dealer. The Western, Central and Southern centers handle the cars at each individual site. Once the cars have been washed & the interior cleaned, they are evaluated and presented on the lot of the Rehab Center. Each car will have an update posted on the window stating the following: mileage, year, make, model, and features, such as air conditioning, power windows, etc. Sealed bids are taken, or an auction is scheduled. The activity of any given Center depends on the number of cars donated and the resident Commander's policy. Most of these Centers do not advertise. The following list of Salvation Army Rehabilitation Centers includes address, phone, and comments about their car sales.

SOUTHERN REGION

ATLANTA, GEORGIA
740 Marietta St., NW
Atlanta, GA 30377-0866
404/ 522-9785
Fax 404/ 522-4523

Uses outside Auction House. Has auction every Thursday night. Open bid. 5-7 cars a week.

AUSTIN, TEXAS
4216 S. Congress
Austin TX 78745
512/ 447-2272
Fax 512/ 326-1272

Advertise- Yes-. Auction Quaterly. 200 cars a year. Lot on facility

BALTIMORE, MARYLAND
2700 W. Patapsco Ave.
Baltimore MD 21227-0584
410/ 525-0530
Fax 410/ 525-0420

BIRMINGHAM, ALABAMA
1401 F. L. Shuttlesworth Dr.
Birmingham AL 35202
205/ 252-8151
Fax 205/ 252-8173

Advertise - no. Auction - no. 1-2 cars a month. Lot on facility.

CHARLOTTE, NORTH CAROLINA
1023 Central Ave.
Charlotte NC 28204
704/ 332-1171
Fax 704/ 332-3345

Advertise - No. 70-80 cars a year. Turns cars to car dealer.

DALLAS/ FORT WORTH
5554 Harry Hines Blvd.
Dallas TX 75235-7213
214/ 630-5611
Fax 214/ 631-6719

Advertise - yes. Auction Quaterly. Open bid. 400-500 cars a year. Lot on facility. They have a Dealer's Licence.

FORT LAUDERDALE, FLORIDA
1901 W. Broward Blvd.
Fort Lauderdale FL 33312-1597
954/ 463-3725
Fax 954/ 761-7891

Advertise - Yes. Auction 3-4 times a year. Open bid.3 - 400 cars a year. Don't sell cars in between.

FORT WORTH, TEXAS
2901 NE 28th St.
Ft. Worth TX 76111-2996
817/ 834-6271
Fax 817/ 831-9514

Advertise - sometimes. Auction every 3 months. 30-40 cars a month. Open bid. Lot on facility.

VIRGINIA BEACH, VIRGINIA
5524 E. Va. Beach Blvd.
Virginia Beach VA 23462
757/ 499-0032
Fax 757/ 499-1427

Advertise - Yes. Flyers. Auction -Yes. 6-8 weeks. 200 Cars a year. Lot on facility.

HOUSTON, TEXAS
1015 Hemhill St.
Houston TX 77007-6113
713/ 869-3551
Fax   713/ 869-7086

Advertise - Yes. Uses Auction House.
150 - 200 cars a year. Open bid.

JACKSONVILLE, FLORIDA
10900 Beach Blvd.
Jacksonville FL32246
904/ 641-2122
Fax   904/ 645-5815

Uses Clearwater Auto Auction.

LITTLE ROCK, ARKANSAS
3618-24 W. Roosevelt Rd.
Little Rock AR 72204—5590
501/ 644-1577
Fax   501/664-8521

Advertise - Yes. Newspaper.
Auction- No. 30- 40 cars a year.
Sealed bid.

LOUISVILLE, KENTUCKY
512 W. Kentucky St.
Louisville KY 40203-3286
502/ 935-6978
Fax   502/ 583-1832

Advertise -Yes. Auction every 3- 4
month. Open bid. 200 cars a year.
Lot on facility.

MEMPHIS, TENNESSEE
130 N. Danny Thomas Blvd.
Memphis TN 38103-1954
901/525-6676
Fax   901/ 576-2285

Advertise - Yes. Uses Auction House
60 cars a year. Lot on facility. Sells a
few cars on their own.

MIAMI, FLORIDA
2236 NW Miami Ct.
Miami FL 33127-4981
305/ 573-4200
Fax   305/ 573-4208

NASHVILLE, TENNESSEE
140 N. First St.
Nashville TN 37213 -1102
P.O. Box 70003
Nashville TN 37207-0003
615/ 259-2348
Fax   615/ 242-4154

Advertise - Yes. Flyers, Newspaper.
Auction Monday, Wednesday,
Friday 8:45 am Open bid .30-40
cars a year. Lot on facility.

NEW ORLEANS, LOUISIANA
200 Jefferson Hwy.
New Orleans LA 70121-2596
504/ 835-1781
Fax 504/ 835-7522

Advertise - Yes. Auction - No. Sells
on a day to day basis .12 cars a
yeek. 300 cars a year. Sealed bid

ALEXANDRIA, VIRGINIA
 (Nothern Virginia Arc)
6528 Little River Turnpike
Alexandria VA 22312
703/642-9270
Fax   703/ 642-3556

Advertise -Yes.Brochures . Uses
Auction House . Open bid. 80- 90
cars a week. 2000 cars a year. Picks
up cars and delivers to Auction
House.

OKLAHOMA CITY, OKLAHOMA
2041 NW 7th St.
Oklahoma City OK 73106-2409
405/ 236-3677
Fax   405/ 232-5841

Advertise - Yes. Newspaper. Auction
Quaterly. 100 cars a year. Open bid.
Lot on facility.

ORLANDO, FLORIDA
3955 W. Colonial Dr.
Orlando FL 32808-7927
407/ 295-9311
Fax 407/ 578-4476

Advertise -Yes. Auction - Yes.
3 times a year. Open bid. Lot on
facility.

RICHMOND, VIRGINIA
2601 Hermitage Rd.
Richmond VA 23220-1199
804/ 359-0269
Fax 8084/ 355-4591

Advertise -Yes. Auction - every
other month. Uses Capital Auto
Auction Inc.:
(800/ 417-6055) 300 cars a week

SAN ANTONIO, TEXAS
1324 S. Flores St.
San Antonio, TX 78204
210/ 233-6877
Fax 210/ 223-4448

Advertise -Yes., flyers, newspaper.
Auction - Yes. 4-5 times a year. 100
cars a year. Lot on facility.

ST. PERTSBURG/ SOUTH BAY, FLORIDA
5885 66th St., N.
St. Petersburg, FL 33709-1597
813/ 625-7781
Fax 813/ 541-5271

Advertise -Yes. Use Clearwater Auto
Auction . 25 cars a month. Pickup
autos deliver to Auction House.

SARASOTA, FLORIDA
2280 17th St.
Sarasota, FL 34234
941/ 954-4549
Fax 941/ 366-0184

Advertise -Yes. Uses Clearwater
Auto Auction . 60-80 cars a year.

TAMPA, FLORIDA
13815 N. Salvation Army Lane
Tampa, FL 33613-2208
813/ 972-0471
Fax 813/ 971-0792

Advertise -Yes. Uses Clearwater
Auto Auction .100-200 cars a year.

TULSA, OKLAHOMA
601-611 N. Main St.
Tulsa, OK 74106-5163
918/ 583-6119
Fax 918/585-3286

Advertise -Yes. Auction - once a
year. 30 cars a year. Open bid. Lot
on facility

BALTIMORE/WASHINGTON DC
&SUBURBAN MARYLAND
3304 Kenilworth Ave.
Bladensburg, MD 20710
301/ 277-7878
Fax 301/ 277-8708

Advertise -Yes. Uses Capitol Auta
Auction.
200 cars a year. Open bid.

WESTERN REGION

ANAHEIM, CALIFORNIA
1300 S. Lewis Street
Anaheim, CA 92005
714/ 750-0414

Advertise - Yes. Auction 2 to 4 times
a year, no sealed bid. 300 cars
donated a year.

BAKERSFIELD, CALIFORNIA
200 Nieteenth St.
Bakersfield, CA 93301
805/ 325-0826

Sealed bid, set out in front.

CANOGA PARK, CALIFORNIA
21375 Roscoe Blvd.
Canoga Park, CA 91304
818/ 893-6321

Advertise - Yes. 30 cars per year
donated. Auction - no. Price is set.

CARPINTERIA, CALIFORNIA
6410 Cindy Lane, P.O. Box 700
Carpinteria, CA 93014-0700
805/ 684-6999

Advertise - Yes, radio and newspaper. 5-10 cars donated per month.
Auction twice a year,
sealed bid, but will sell anytime. Lot
on facility.

COLORADO SPRINGS, COLORADO
505 So. Weber Street
Colorado Springs, CO 80901
719-473-6161

Advertise - No. 3-4 donated a year.
Auction - no, sealed bid. Lot on
facility.

DENVER, COLORADO
4751 Broadway
P.O. Box 16024,80216
Denver, CO 80216
303/ 294-0027

Doesn't sell to public. Sells to local
dealer. 2 cars donated a month.

FRESNO, CALIFORNIA
804 So. Parallel Ave.
Fresno, CA 93721
209/ 237-7121

Advertise - Yes, depending on the car. 2-3 a month donated. Sealed bid. Lot on facility.

LONG BEACH, CALIFORNIA
1370 Alamitos Ave.
Long Beach, CA
310/ 210-2355

Advertise - Yes. 2 cars per week, 50-60 a year donated. Sealed bid. Lot on facility.

HEALDSBURG, CALIFORNIA
200 Lytton Springs Road
P.O. Box 660
Healdsburg, CA 95440-0660
707/ 433-3334

Advertise - Yes. 15-20 cars a month donated. Auction last Saturday of every month. Open to sealed bid. Lot on facility.

OAKLAND, CALIFORNIA
601 Webster St.
P.O. Box 24054
Oakland, CA 94307

Advertise - No, word of mouth. 15-20 a month donated. Silent auction, min. bids 1:00-2:00 pm Mon. - Fri. Lot on facility.

PASADENA, CALIFORNIA
56 W. Del Mar
Pasadena, CA 91105
818/ 795-8075

Advertise - Yes, throughout the Western region. 50 cars donated a year. Auction - Yes. Sealed bid. Lot on facility.

PERRIS, CALIFORNIA
24201 Orange Ave.
P.O. Box 278
Perris, CA 92570

Advertise - some, in Pennysaver. 2-3 cars donated a month. Sealed bid. Park out front on street.

PHOENIX, ARIZONA
625 S. Central Ave.
P.O. Box 20547;85036
Phoenix, AZ 85004
602/ 256-4500

Advertise - No. 30 cars a year donated. Auction - No. Sealed bid. Lot across the street.

PORTLAND, OREGON
139 S.E. Martin Luther King Jr. Blvd
Portland, OR 97214-1193
503/ 235-4192

Advertise - Yes. 6-7 cars donated per month. Auction every other month. Open and sealed bid.

SACRAMENTO, CALIFORNIA
1615 D Street
P.O. Box 2940
Sacramento, CA 95814
916/ 441-5267

Advertise - No. 20 cars per year
donated. Auction - No. Sealed bid.
Lot on facility.

SAN BERNADINO, CALIFORNIA
363 S. Doolittle Rd.
San Bernardino, CA 92408
909/ 889-9604

Advertise - No. 12-20 donated per
year. Auction - Yes. Sealed bid. Lot
on facility.

SAN DIEGO, CALIFORNIA
1335 Broadway
San Diego, CA 92101
619/ 239-4037

Advertise - Yes, in Auto Trader and
the Internet. 200 cars donated per
year. Auction - bidding system.

SAN FRANCISCO, CALIFORNIA
1500 Valencia St.
San Francisco, CA 94110-4409
415/ 695-8000

Advertise - No. 60-70 cars donated
a year. Auction - No. Estimate a
min. price, sealed bid.
 Lot on facility.

SAN JOSE, CALIFORNIA
702 W. Taylor St.
San Jose, CA 95126
408/ 298-7600

Advertise - Yes. 800-900 cars donated a year. Auction - No. Sealed
bid. Lot on facility.

SEATTLE, WASHINGTON
1000 4TH Ave. S.
Seattle, Washington 98134
206/ 507-0503

 Advertise -No. Auction - No. Sealed
bid system.

STOCKTON, CALIFORNIA
1247 S. Wilson Way
Stockton, Ca 95205-7096
209/ 466-3071

Advertise - No. 75-100 Cars A Year.
Auction - Yes. Sealed bid and post
price. Lot on facility.

TACOMA, WASHINGTON
409 Puyallup Ave.
Tacoma, WA 90421
206/ 627-8118

Advertise - Yes. 15 cars donated a
month. 60-70 per year. Auction -
Yes. Sealed bid.
Gated lot across the street.

TUSCON, ARIZONA
2717 S. 6th Ave.
P.O. Box 7729
Tuscon, AZ 85713
520/ 624-1741

Advertise - Some, other donations
are included. 30 cars donated per
year. Auctions - Yes.
Closed bid. Lot on facility.

VAN NUYS, CALIFORNIA
6059 Van Nuys Blvd.
Van Nuys, California 91401
818/ 778-1177
Advertise. Auction

CENTRAL REGION

CHICAGO, ILLINOIS
506 N. Des Plaines Steet
Chicago, IL 60610
312/ 738-4367
Fax 312/ 738-5731

Advertise - No. Cars only on
Thursday. Lot on facility.

FLINT, MICHIGAN
2200 N. Dort Highway
Flint, MI 48506
810/ 234-2678
Fax 810/ 234-1439

Advertise - No. Few cars occasionally.

CHICAGO, ILLINOIS
2258 Clybourn Ave.
Chicago, IL 60614
773/ 477-1300
Fax 773/ 477-1678

Advertise - No. Come by lot on facility.

GARY, INDIANA
1351 Eleventh Ave.
Gary, IN 46402
219/ 882-9377
Fax 219/ 882-3309

Advertise - No. Few cars occasionally. Lot on facility.

DAVENPORT, IOWA
Davenport, IA 52808-3726
319/ 232-2748
Fax 319/ 232-7862

Advertise - No. Come by lot on facility.

INDIANAPOLIS, INDIANA
711 E. Washington Street
Indianapolis, IN 46202
317/ 638-6585
Fax 317/ 685-2461

Advertise - No. Few cars occasionally. Lot on facility. Open bid.

DES MOINES, IOWA
133 E. Second Street
Des Moines, IA 50303
515/ 243-4277
FAX 515/ 243-8636

Advertise - No. Few cars occasionally.

LINCOLN, NEBRASKA
737 "P" Street
Lincoln, NE 68506
402/474-4747

Couple of cars each year.

MILWAUKEE, WISCONSIN
342 N. Jackson Street
Milwaukee, WI 53202
414/276-4316

Few cars each year. Sealed bids.

MINNEAPOLIS, MINNESOTA
900 N. Fourth Street
Minneapolis, MN 55401
612/332-5855

Advertise - No. Sealed bid.

OMAHA, NEBRASKA
2501 Center Street
Omaha, NE 68105
402/342-4135

Few cars. Sealed bid.

PONTIAC, MICHIGAN
118 W. Lawrence Street
Pontiac, MI 48341
810/338-9601

No advertising. Uses American
Auto Sales in Monroe, MI - 313-722-
1010 Set price.

ROCKFORD, ILLINOIS
1706 18th Avenue
Rockford, IL 61104
815/397-0440

No advertising. Dozen cars per
year. Set price.

ROMULUS, MICHIGAN
5931 Middlebelt Road
Romulus, MI 48174
313/729-3939

Displays on lot. Set price.

ST. LOUIS, MISSOURI
3949 Forest Park Blvd.
St. Louis, MO 63108
314/535-0057

No advertising. Couple dozen cars
per year. Set prices.

SOUTH BEND, INDIANA
510-518 South Main Street
South Bend, IN 46601
219/288-2539

WAUKEGAN, ILLINOIS
431 S. Genesee Street
Waukegan, IL 60085
847/662-7730

No advertising. Sells off the
lot to interested buyer.

WICHITA, KANSAS
3601 N. St. Francis Street
Wichita, KS 67219
316/832-0247

A boat or car infrequently. Sealed
bid.

EASTERN REGION

This region routes all donated cars to one auction house in Philadelphia, Pennsylvania. Approximately 250 cars per auction, specifically identified as Salvation Army donations, are auctioned off every Wednesdays at the following auction house:

Capital Auto Auction
1-888-515-4222

National Charities

The local chapters of many national charities are holding auctions on an annual basis in every large to medium-sized community in the US.

Here is a list of national charities that you will want to check out:

Cystic Fibrosis   Muscular Dystrophy
Heart & Lung Association   Multiple Sclerosis
Cancer Society
Red Cross

Other Charities

Smaller, local organizations, such as symphonies, art museums, historical and natural museums, homeless shelters and Hospice groups, private schools, child abuse and battered women's centers, youth athletic teams, and smaller interest groups within public schools, all of these use auctions to raise money.

How to Find Charity Auctions

Look in white pages of your phone book for the local chapter of each of these charities. Call them and ask if they hold regular auctions. If so, ask when and where their next scheduled auction will take place.

Consult you local television cable company. Ask which channel the public service announcements are listed on. By federal law, cable companies must provide the towns and cities they service with a "bulletin board" free of charge to all local, not for profit organizations. These listings often take the form of a "crawl" — much like the program information channel — repeating about every five minutes. The free listings, or public service announcements are submitted by local charities and non-profit cultural groups. They describe, in detail, upcoming functions, events and fund raising activities.

Keep your eyes and ears open. Most Americans have an aversion to advertising in newspapers, and they often ignore posters and flyers pasted up in store windows. But if you want to make sure you don't miss a really great auction, start noticing the odd ad and the small poster. As with cable companies, local newspapers provide either free, or at a reduced rate, listings of various charitys' upcoming events. Check both your daily and weekly newspapers for their calendar of events that can be easily found and consulted for time, place, and might even include what to expect in terms of goods.

All non-profit or charity organizations have free access to the local cable TV bulletin board. This is a running list you can easily find by calling your cable company and asking which channel broadcasts this information.

Find the professional auctioneers near you. Let them know what you are looking for. They will be happy to keep your name in their records and mail you a flier to let you know about upcoming sales and special treasures. This way you'll know about upcoming charity auctions, as well as other regular auctions.

The Truth About Charity Auctions

In both national charities and small community charities, the following truisms apply:

- The items are generally donated by well-meaning, generous, and often wealthy individuals who want to help the charity reach its goals and be successful.

- Because putting on an auction costs the organization so little, and the benefits are so great, there is an atmosphere of excitement and expectation at these events — and everyone comes away from the auction having won!

• BEST OF ALL — Nobody in the organization wants to deal with leftover items the next day. That means the charity has a huge incentive for making sure the bidding on items begins low enough to spark and insure a sale. For this reason many auction organizers will instruct the auctioneer to keep the bidding reasonable, and, in the case of no bids, to lower the starting figure until someone shows interest.

Goods & Services at a Bargain Price

Most charities send their volunteers out in droves to local businesses, and even to non-profit theater and music groups, to ask for donations. Contributing to a charity is good advertising for any business or group, and therefore, provides a great opportunity for individuals looking for real deals. In other words, <u>countless bargains are to be had for the bidding</u>. Often, goods and services that will not be found at an estate auction, or an antique house auction, can be readily obtained. Extraordinary and useful items can include such things as $100 worth of printing at the local copy store, which can be gotten for $50, or a cruise to Hawaii for half the going rate. Other success stories we've witnessed are the winning bid for a fully organized hiking vacation for four teenagers which was donated by an experienced camper came in at $200; two round-trip tickets to New York City (donated by a businessman with too many frequent flyer miles) won with a bid of $500; two nights in a local luxury hotel (won for half the rate); dinner for four at a favorite restaurant with a famous chef ($90); a pair of season tickets to an award winning theater (half price).

Consignments

This is definitely a case of <u>BUYER BEWARE.</u> Sometimes a charity will take items on consignment from local car dealers, fur coat merchants, or antique shops. The store owner makes a deal with the charity that he must receive a certain dollar figure in return for his donation. Anything the auction brings in above that figure, the charity keeps. Try to find out which items, if any, are under consignment. The chances of getting a really great bargain can be significantly less. Several auctioneers interviewed for this chapter told us they refuse to be involved with consignments, stating that it makes the whole auction process more complicated, and less straightforward than it should be.

Unusual Items

Charity auctions will often contain very unusual items, especially if celebrities have donated to the charity. We once bought a famous golfer's PGA tournament score card to give to an avid golfer. He was thrilled to receive the card as a birthday present. The price was $20, but worth much more to us and to him. Years ago, a close friend bid on Shirley Temple's dresses at a Milk Fund auction and won for her three daughters five charming 1940's frocks (actually worn by the famous child star) that they played dress-up in for many years. Friends have found amazing treasures at these charity sales, such as authentic antique china and furniture. Leaded crystal ashtrays, figurines, even old magazines can be bid on without a lot of competition and won for a very reasonable price. Generally speaking, the wealthier the community, the greater chance of finding treasure. The great news is you don't have to be wealthy to attend, or to bid!

Collectibles Newsletters

Nearly every collectable item has a trade magazine, or newsletter that can be subscribed to for very little cost, if any fee is charged at all. You can find these publications by asking your local auctioneer or antiques dealer. Just ask the dealer or merchant who carries something like what you want. For instance, if rare books is your thing, ask a rare book dealer what publications advertise rare book auctions and sales. Become a subscriber to any number of newsletters so you can be among the first to know what's out there and where to go to get it!

FINDING GREAT BUYS IN HIDDEN PLACES

Mini-storage and Moving Company Auctions

The mini-storage industry has grown by leaps and bounds in the past five years. You can look around and find such facilities in nearly every town and city. And they come in all shapes and sizes — both national chains and smaller "mom & pop" types.

Whatever the size, storage unit owners face an ongoing and huge dilemma: Every year hundreds of mini-storage customers stop paying their rent. Large moving companies, too, end up with boxes of goods that go unclaimed, but which take up valuable space. The only way these businesses can recoup on their costs is by holding a public auction to sell the items in the units. Sometimes the contents are auctioned off sight unseen. Sometimes the units are opened at the time of the bidding. Some storage places offer a preview the day before. The sight-unseen auction is a lot of fun, and because it's understood that the bidder is taking a big chance, the bidding is kept low — as the mini-storage owner is happy to recoup a month's rent and have the space available again. We've seen some instances where the contents were quite valuable, including such things as jewelry, antiques, and even weapons. Don't count on finding a sack full of money, but it has been known to happen.

Generally speaking, mini-storage facilities and moving companies auction off the contents of delinquent units every month or two. The truth is, they can't wait to get rid of the stuff (referred to as chattel by storage owners), so they can rent the unit to a paying customer.

Read your local newspaper and the newspapers in neighboring communities to find the time and place of upcoming storage facility auctions. If all the details you want to know are not mentioned, like whether or not there is a preview of the items, or if items will be auctioned off one at a time or by the complete unit, then call the number in the ad and ask.

If a phone number is not listed in the newspaper ad, consult the yellow pages of your local phone book. If you can't find any ads in the newspaper, use the phone book to find the locations and phone numbers of the mini-storage and moving companies in your community. Call them and ask when their next auction is scheduled, and while you have them on the phone, ask how they plan to conduct the auction.

Safety Deposit Box Contents Auctions

These auctions are held by reputable auction companies who deal with banks and other businesses that rent out safety deposit boxes. The contents of unclaimed safety deposit boxes are generally delivered by the auction company to a hotel ballroom or other large hall, in "evidence bags." The bags are opened and the items displayed for preview one or two days prior to the actual auction.

As often as not, the contents belongs to someone who died without a will. Many, many treasures are to be had for the right bid — often expensive items that would cost far more in a store.

The best way to find out about such auctions is to consult Volume II of this program. Call and ask the auction houses nearest you if they hold auctions of safety deposit box contents. If so, ask to be put on the mailing list.

Important Tips for the Bidder from Certified Auctioneers

Several auctioneers, some graduates from the Certified Auctioneers Institute, were consulted for this chapter. They see all kinds of people coming to auctions, and were eager to pass on what they see as the profile of the successful bidder. Here are their suggestions:

Do your homework. We know we've said this earlier in the book, but it can't be emphasized enough. In order to get real deals, whether a car, a service, or a piece of china, you must know the price that the item would fetch in a reputable antique shop or store. You can "shop" to find out this necessary information, or you can call an antique dealer or store owner in your area to ask the prices of particular brands, makes and models.

Know what you can afford. In order to avoid Post Purchase Depression, it is important that you go into any auction with a "top figure" that you are willing to spend, and can afford to spend. Don't go over that amount unless you can deal with the consequences or think you can resell the item for a higher price than you paid.

Avoid getting caught up in a competitive bidding war. This is not about your worth as a person. If someone out-bids you, fine. There's always the next sale.

Get what you deserve. Check out every item you can <u>up close and personal.</u> The worst case scenario is this: You bid on and win something you want, only to find out later that it doesn't work, or has a crack or flaw that makes it unusable and worth less than you paid. It's only in rare instances that a charity will refund your money for an item you discover is not up to par. We have found that businesses, however, never refund, as it is understood from the top that you're winning bid means you buy it, you keep it. In fact, at some auctions, you must sign a paper stating that you agree all winning bids are final.

Remember there's a learning curve. Just like everything else, bidding at auction and getting good deals takes some time in order to be proficient. Be willing to start small while you're watching the more experienced bidders. You can learn from them and you can learn from yourself. The more you attend auctions of any kind, the better bidder you will become, and the more successful your purchases.

Go to have fun!! Auctions can be very lively, often comic and dramatic, and therefore, extremely exciting. It's a great way to spend a few hours. Who knows, you may find the exact thing you've been looking for, or something you've never thought of will be there on the preview table that you realize instantly will make your life complete.

Chapter 19:
Ready, Set, Go!!!

> "If you are a genius and unsuccessful, everybody treats you as if you were a genius, but when you come to be successful, when you commence to earn money, when you are really successful, then your family and everybody no longer treats you like a genius, they treat you like a man who has become successful."
>
> Pablo Picasso (1881–1973)

You're well on your way to becoming one of thousands of people across the country who enjoy the excitement and satisfaction from buying at auctions. Whether you are looking for a bargain on your next car, starting a business of selling surplus property you have acquired at auctions, or simply looking for a fun and exciting way to spend your weekends, you're off to a great start.

We have provided you with a wealth of information on many different types of auctions. You now have a good understanding of how an auction works, the types of items you can expect to find at auctions, and how to place bids at an auction. Your Volume 2 listing provides dates and locations of hundreds of upcoming auctions across the country. In addition, Volume 1 gives the phone numbers and addresses to contact to have your name placed on mailing lists so you can continually be notified of upcoming auctions in your area.

Please let us know of your successes. We would like to include them in future listings. In appreciation we will send you a complimentary copy of our next Volume 2 auction listing. We look forward to hearing of the bargains you have successfully acquired at auctions!

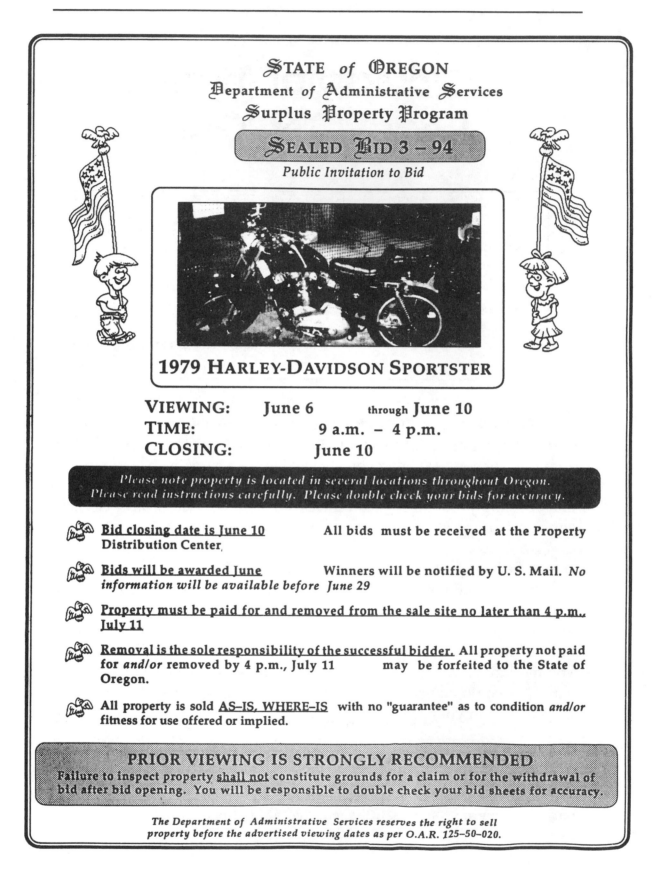

STATE of OREGON
Department of Administrative Services
Surplus Property Program

SEALED BID 3 – 94

Public Invitation to Bid

1979 HARLEY-DAVIDSON SPORTSTER

VIEWING: June 6   through **June 10**

TIME: 9 a.m. – 4 p.m.

CLOSING: June 10

Please note property is located in several locations throughout Oregon. Please read instructions carefully. Please double check your bids for accuracy.

- **Bid closing date is June 10**   All bids must be received at the Property Distribution Center,

- **Bids will be awarded June**   Winners will be notified by U. S. Mail. *No information will be available before* June 29

- **Property must be paid for and removed from the sale site no later than 4 p.m., July 11**

- **Removal is the sole responsibility of the successful bidder.** All property not paid for *and/or* removed by 4 p.m., July 11   may be forfeited to the State of Oregon.

- All property is sold **AS–IS, WHERE–IS** with no "guarantee" as to condition *and/or* fitness for use offered or implied.

PRIOR VIEWING IS STRONGLY RECOMMENDED

Failure to inspect property **shall not** constitute grounds for a claim or for the withdrawal of bid after bid opening. You will be responsible to double check your bid sheets for accuracy.

The Department of Administrative Services reserves the right to sell property before the advertised viewing dates as per O.A.R. 125–50–020.

Glossary of Terms

Absolute Auction:

This is just another term for an auction with no reserve, meaning there is no set dollar amount where the bidding needs to begin. The highest bidder wins. These auctions are highly attractive to the buyer because they truly can find terrific bargains. They are also a test of the auctioneer's marketing and sales ability. He needs to get a big crowd so that there is competitive bidding.

An absolute auction is an auction in its truest sense. The auctioneer knows this—and so does the public. For obvious reasons, it is not always the most popular with the individual trying to get top dollar for their merchandise.

You will sometimes see ads in the paper which say: **ABSOLUTE AUCTION***. The asterisk indicates you need to look for the fine print elsewhere in the ad. What you will find in that fine print is that only SOME of the items are being offered in this manner.

Why would an auctioneer advertise in this way? It's simple—because absolute auctions draw huge crowds of people who bid like crazy. This is the auctioneer's dream, so he will try to make every auction look as appealing to the prospective buyers as possible.

Something you always need to keep in mind is that the auctioneer is playing both ends against the middle. It's his job! He has to satisfy both the seller and the buyer, which we all know is no easy task.

If you run across an auction which is advertised in this manner, give the auctioneer a call and find out exactly what items will be sold in the absolute auction manner.

Appraisal:

The appraised value of an item is the amount which the item is thought to be worth. Before selling an old painting, for example, you might take it to an art dealer for an appraisal. The appraisal will then give you an idea of how much to ask for it. When considering buying an expensive item of jewelry, antiques, artwork or collectibles, you would be well advised to first have them appraised by a professional to make sure you aren't paying well over their appraised value.

However, you also want to remember that the value of an item is only what someone else is willing to pay for it. Even though you may have a fur coat that is appraised at $2,000, sometimes in selling an item you may have to accept less because you can't find a buyer willing to pay that price.

Along the same vein, sometimes at an auction certain items may have been previously appraised and assigned a 'reserve' price. The reserve price is typically 25-50% less than the appraised value. This gives the auctioneer a point at which to start the bidding. At the auction, the auctioneer is very much 'at the mercy' of the bidders. Many times an item will only sell for what the market will bear, as the bidders (YOU) set the prices.

As-Is:

Most auction catalogs and flyers tell you that all items are sold "as-is, where-is". This means the items are to be sold exactly as you see them, with no warranty or guarantee that they are in working order. This is why you are well advised to attend the auction previews and examine the items you are interested in bidding on. Make sure you start the engine and examine as well as is possible any vehicle you want to purchase. "Where-is" means that you are responsible for transporting any item(s) you buy; the auctioneer is not going to have them delivered to you.

"Auction Fever":

Let's be honest, attending an auction is EXCITING. The air is filled with electricity! Everyone there wants to go home with a steal. It's easy to get caught up in the excitement and go wild with your bidding. Suddenly you find yourself bidding $50 for a dresser that you had decided you wouldn't pay over $35 for. You've got a case of "auction fever".

The easiest way of avoiding coming down with a case of "auction fever" is to set a limit to what you will bid for an item BEFORE the bidding starts. Make notes when you are previewing the items, and then stick with your previously-set limits. Remember—the reason you are attending an auction in the first place is to SAVE MONEY.

In setting your $ limits, you may want to consider two things: the amount you hope to pay for the item, and the most you will pay for the item. Also, it's good to remember how important the item is to you. If you are bidding on an antique or collectible that you REALLY want to add to your own private collection, you can probably set your limit a bit higher than you would if you were just purchasing the item to resell.

Auction With Reserve:

The term 'reserve' means having a limitation. So in this instance, when an auction has a reserve, the items must be sold at or above a specific price. This clause is more a PR tool than a practice for the governmental agencies. It assists them in defending themselves against charges of giving everything away too cheaply.

Bid:

An offer of payment for merchandise. When you bid $20 for a lamp, you are making an offer of $20 for that lamp. The auctioneer will then see if someone else wants to bid more money for the lamp. If no one else bids more than your $20 bid, you are the successful bidder.

Bid Deposit:

Typically when sending in a sealed bid on an item you will be required to include a cashier's check as a bid deposit. The auction notice will specify the amount of bid deposit required (for example, 10% of your bid). This is to screen out people who aren't really serious about purchasing the item. If your bid isn't accepted, the bid deposit is automatically returned. If you have the winning bid, then to claim your new property you will need to come up with the remainder of the balance due (in this example, the additional 90%).

Bidder's Number:

This is the number given to you when you register at many public auctions. This identifies you as a bidder and authorizes you to bid. Since this number has been assigned to YOU personally, do not lose it or idly drop it on the floor. You are responsible for any bid made with that number. When you pay for the items you successfully bid on, you may again be asked for identification or to show your bidder's number to verify that you are the rightful new owner of the particular auction merchandise. In Chapter 2.0 Understanding Auctions we show you a reduced (smaller) copy of a bidder's number that we were issued at a recent auction.

"Big Ticket" Item:

This is simply any single item that sells for a large amount of money. As an example, a filing cabinet is not a "big ticket" item; a new car is. We generally consider a "big ticket" item to be something that costs over $1000.

"Blue Book":

The "Blue Book" is a frequently used automobile buying guide. The "Blue Book" is used as a guide to give you an idea of what a particular car may be worth. If you see a car you are interested in bidding on listed in an auction catalog you can look up its "Blue Book" price to see what it might sell for 'on the street'. Knowing ahead of time what a car is worth is invaluable to you when you are bidding at auction. In Chapter 16.0 we provide you with the address to subscribe to the National Automobile Dealer's Used Car Guide, along with many other guides. You may also be able to check out the "Blue Book" at your local library or purchase one at a local bookstore.

Buyer's Premium:

At the majority of public auctions there will not be a commission, or buyer's premium, due. This means that the amount you bid is the amount you pay. However, at auctions conducted by commercial auctioneers, the auction notice may indicate that a buyer's premium will be added. The buyer's premium is added on to the amount of the successful bid, and is basically a commission for the auctioneer. For example, you attend an auction where there is a 2% buyer's premium, and you are the successful bidder on a table for $10. The 2% buyer's premium adds 20 cents to the price of your table, so your total purchase price is $10.20. Your auction catalog will indicate whether or not a buyer's premium will be charged, but if you're in doubt, make sure you ask ahead of time.

Cashier's Check:

A check issued by a bank. Sometimes at an auction you must pay for your items with a cashier's check instead of a personal check. You must go to a bank in order to have a cashier's check issued.

Catalog:

The auction catalog provides you with a list of the items available for auction along with their descriptions, quantities, and lot numbers. The catalog will also give you the Terms of Sale and other information. Always read your catalog thoroughly before making a bid.

Condition of Merchandise

Can vary from "new" to "salvage." Remember that at almost every auction the merchandise is sold "as-is", so be sure to inspect it first. The merchandise descriptions in the catalogs are approximate and the merchandise carries no guarantee that it is in working order. Again, at the auction preview always inspect any item(s) you are planning on bidding on.

Contraband:

Contraband is smuggled goods that are forbidden by law to be imported or exported to or from the United States. Most types of contraband that have been confiscated are destroyed by the Customs Service. Occasionally an item of contraband will be auctioned off instead of destroyed. In most cases this will be something like furs.

Customs Service:

The U.S. Customs Service is a branch of the U.S. government. The Customs Service auctions are currently handled by E. G. & G. Dynatrend. At Customs Service auctions various types of property are sold, including automobiles, aircraft, boats, electronic equipment, jewelry, clothing and real estate. This is primarily property that has been seized by the Customs Service. All proceeds generated through the sales of this seized property are transferred to the U.S. Treasury.

Default:

If you fail to comply with the payment or removal specifications listed in the Terms of Sale at a particular auction then you are considered to be in default. If you are found to be in default then any right or title you have acquired in the merchandise will be lost, the property reverts back to the previous owner (usually the government) and any payments you have made are forfeited.

Deposits:

Many times when you purchase a "big ticket" item that you are not taking home that day you will be required to leave a deposit. This helps to guarantee that you will be back to pay the remainder and pick up the item the following day or within the time period allowed in the Terms of Sale.

DoD:

The Department of Defense. Chapter 14.0 of this directory provides you with information on the Department of Defense auctions.

Errata Sheets:

When there have been changes made to the auction catalog after it has been published then errata sheets will commonly be inserted. These list any changes or corrections to the auction catalog.

Export Only:

Some merchandise sold at U.S. Customs Service auctions will be marked "For Export Only". This means that this particular merchandise cannot be registered, used, or resold in the United States. It must be exported from the U.S. within a particular time frame (which will be found in the auction catalog under the Terms of Sale).

Flyer:

An auction advertisement that provides information on an upcoming auction. The flyers typically advise you of date, times, location, preview date and times, some of the items available for auction, and also sometimes list the Terms of Sale.

Government Surplus:

Basically any items the government has purchased and no longer has a use for. This can vary tremendously, from used vehicles to office equipment to sleeping bags. I have a flyer for an upcoming government surplus sale by the Department of Defense in front of me. Some of the items listed for sale include typewriters, office furniture, saddles, clothing, cameras, tools, electrical equipment, pumps, television sets, copy machines, vacuum cleaners, computer equipment, hardware, boots, pool tables, generators, ammunition, ice machines, paint sprayers, tents, ladders, riding lawn mowers, engines, soap, washers and dryers, refrigerators, scrap metal, cargo trailers, flatbed trailers, tires, vehicles, and even mobile homes. And even though an item is classified as surplus this does NOT mean that it has been used. Many times you will find brand new items that are simply not needed and so are classified as surplus.

GSA:

The General Services Administration. This agency was created to manage government property and records. They are in charge of supervising the construction and operation of government buildings. They also purchase and distribute the supplies used by the Federal government. In Chapter 13.0 we provide you with information on attending GSA auctions.

Hand Signals:

Each of us has heard horror stories of someone at an auction scratching their nose and ending up buying something they weren't even bidding on. This is probably one of the most scary elements to the auction newcomer—"What if I make the wrong move and they think I'm bidding?" Unless you're attending an art auction, it's unlikely that scratching your nose, tugging your ear or wiping your face would ever be accepted as hand signals.

Hand signals are used a lot to place bids at an auction, but they are usually as simple as raising your hand to indicate your accepting a bid. If you are worried about the possibility of confusion, make sure you put your bidder's number in your pocket or purse. If the auctioneer can't see your bidder's number, they won't accept a bid.

More experienced attendees may use hand signals such as waving their hand horizontally to or from their chest (this would indicate to the auctioneer that the bidder wants to cut the increments in half). There are multitudes of hand and body signals you may see when you attend auctions. As you become more familiar with the sales methods, terms and general theme of auctions, you may wish to bid in a like manner. For the time being, don't ever forget to keep your bidder's number hidden from view until you are actively bidding.

Increments:

An increment is the dollar spread between bids. The increment depends upon the size of the property or merchandise being sold and the hesitancy of two or more bidders to bid any higher. Every bid on a car might increase by $100 (this would be a $100 increment) or it may only increase by $25 (a $25 increment). Increments are decided between bidders and the auctioneer during the course of the auction. Auctioneers often speed up the auction by asking for $100 increments for a bid. If he/she sees bidders dropping out, the bid increment may be dropped to $50 to keep more bidders participating. At the onset, the pace is usually set by the auctioneer. As the auction proceeds, the bidders can change the pace by slowing down on their bidding, which in turn forces the auctioneer to back off and decrease the increments.

Knockdown:

This term refers to the end of a sale. It originated when auctioneers used hammers to indicate that a successful bid had been received. They would knock on the podium so the crowd would know an item had been sold. The gavel or hammer is still used at many auctions. If the auctioneer isn't using one of these, he or she will point to the bidder and shout "SOLD",

The knockdown price is what the bidder has agreed to pay for the auctioned item.

Lien:

A lien (pronounced "lean") is a legal claim on another's property as security for the payment of a debt. A lienholder has the right to take and hold or to sell the property of a borrower who defaults on a loan. If you borrow money from someone to buy a car and put up your stereo to secure the loan, and later you default on the loan, the person you borrowed money from has the right to sell your stereo to help recover the money you borrowed. Rarely there will be property at auction (usually only IRS auctions) that may be subject to a lien. This means there is money owed on an item in addition to the amount you bid. This doesn't happen very often, but is another good reason to always read the auction catalog carefully, as it will tell if there is a lien on an item up for auction.

Lot:

A grouping of merchandise to be sold as a unit. A lot may contain only one item or may contain 100 items. Usually similar items are grouped together to form a lot, but not always. Make sure you get an auction catalog and also preview the lots before deciding on a particular lot to bid on.

Marshals Service, U.S.:

The U.S. Marshals Service is a branch of the U.S. Justice Department. The Marshals Service auctions commonly contain items seized during drug raids and also forfeited property that has been taken from convicted criminals. In Chapter 9.0 we give you information on attending auctions conducted by the Marshals Service.

Minimum Bid:

Government agencies are often fond of having a minimum bid at their public auctions. The minimum bid is the lowest acceptable bid allowed by the auctioneer. Bids can only go up from this point. If no one makes the minimum bid, the auction of that item stops.

This is not a very popular auction practice, and in some instances keeps people from participating. A smart auctioneer knows he/she will get their minimum bid or more once the auction is under way. A good auctioneer will get much more than his minimum bid if he works the crowd.

Notice of Award:

The Notice of Award (NOA) is the receipt for a purchase. The Notice of Award is given at the time payment is made. You will be asked to show your Notice of Award before the items you purchased will be released to you.

Opening Bid:

This is where the auction starts. The opening bid is an offer to buy an item at a specific price. The opening bid may be less than the minimum bid—or more.

The auctioneer can ask for a price on a piece of merchandise being auctioned, but the bidders don't have to take him up on this offer. A bidder can always counter with a lower price—an important point you should keep in mind!

Paddle:

A paddle is simply a bidder's number on a paddle that resembles a Ping-Pong paddle. It's basically a bidder's number with a convenient handle.

PAL:

See "Public Action Line" below.

Payment:

Acceptable methods of payment at an auction will be clearly spelled out under the Terms of Sale. These can include cash, personal check, cashier's check, business check, and credit cards. Not all methods of payment are allowed at all auctions. Some may specify cash or check with a bank's letter of credit only. Make sure you read the Terms of Sale before the day of the auction so you are able to pay for the purchases you wish to make.

Personal Property:

Basically personal property can be defined as anything that is not real property (meaning real estate). This can cover anything from airplanes to zebras, but does not include land.

Public Auction Line (PAL):

This is a recorded telephone message system that provides information on upcoming auctions of the U.S. Customs Service. These auctions are currently handled by E. G. & G. Dynatrend. The Public Auction Line is accessible 24 hours a day by dialing (703) 351-7887. You are then asked to press the number associated with the topic you are interested in hearing about. We provide more information on PAL for you in Chapter 12.

Real Property:

Real property is another term for real estate, which is land. This may or may not include buildings or improvements. Sometimes real estate offered at auction may be a parcel of land with a house on it, sometimes it may be a commercial building, other times it may be an unimproved lot or acreage. Real property includes office buildings, houses, apartments, retail stores, condominiums, and even golf courses.

Reserve Price:

See "Auction with Reserve".

Salvage:

Items sold as salvage are sold only for their scrap value. Salvage items are usually only of interest to scrap dealers and recyclers, someone who is already set up to take advantage of its value as scrap material.

Sealed Bid:

Sealed bids are bids submitted in a sealed envelope either in person or by registered mail. Sometimes sealed bids are required to be submitted on a particular form. It is not uncommon for a deposit to be required with your sealed bid. This is intended to screen out everyone except the really serious bidders. Sealed bids are all opened together at the appointed time. The successful bidder is notified that he has the winning bid, and all other bid deposits are returned. When a sealed bid is submitted for an item at a public auction it will be the opening bid.

Seized Property:

This defines property confiscated by a Customs or law enforcement officer when laws have been violated.

Spot Bid:

At this type of auction the bidders are usually required to attend in person. Items are offered as usual, but instead of making a verbal bid the bidders write their offer on a written form. The bids are collected, and the highest bidder is announced publicly.

Subject To:

Another way to say "auction with reserve" is to say "subject to seller's confirmation". This gives the seller a chance to back out of the sale if they don't think the final bid is high enough.

While this is not a common practice, it is used by auctioneers when they have a seller who has some doubts about whether they really want to sell items at auction. Since reserve auctions aren't popular with the public, this allows the auctioneer to make a compromise with his client without alienating the public.

Since the seller will have to pay a fee for the auction when it is over, whether they allow items to be sold or not, they generally allow a sale to go through.

Another "subject to" clause you may see in the Conditions of Sale is "subject to court confirmation". You are most likely to see this wording at a bankruptcy or estate auction, since the judge has to approve a sale before it's final.

The odds of this being enforced are very slight. I was personally involved in a restaurant bankruptcy several years ago. While the terms and conditions of sale had this clause, the majority of the equipment was successfully purchased for about 10 cents on the dollar. The judge didn't even blink.

What you have to remember when attending business bankruptcy auctions is that the individuals conducting the sale generally know very little about the business that has gone bankrupt. While they may have a few guidelines on which equipment is the most valuable, they tend not to have a very good overview. Again, I will refer to the restaurant bankruptcy just to give you some good examples of what I'm talking about.

The restaurant had lots of neon lighting which was put on the auction block. The fixtures were less than a year old and had cost $4,500. They sold at auction for $50.00. There was a wine collection worth $5,000 which sold for $250. A walk-in cooler/freezer worth $5,000 that still looked brand new was sold for less than $1,000. The booths and tables were sold for about $196.

So, as you can see, the bankruptcy trustee couldn't have been paying too much attention to this sale. The simple reason being that he probably had little, if any, idea of the value.

On the other side of the coin, allowing this equipment to be sold so inexpensively allowed someone else to be able to get started in a business with very little outlay of capital.

When you are attending bankruptcy or estate auctions, you should ask the auctioneer about any "subject to" clauses you have seen in the Conditions of Sale. He will have a clearer understanding of the seller's or trustee's leanings with regard to the property or merchandise being sold. Then you can make an intelligent decision on whether or not to bid.

Terms and Conditions:

The Terms and Conditions should be detailed in the auction catalog, and provide information on such things as method of payment, removal of property, deposits, and other auction-specific details. Terms and Conditions are unique to each auction. For example, one auction you attend may accept credit cards as a method of payment, while the next auction you attend may be cash only. Make sure you read the Terms and Conditions before bidding on an item. If you have any questions regarding the Terms and Conditions it is best to ask the auctioneer before the start of the auction.

Upset Price:

This is the price which must be reached before a sale is valid. Auctions with reserve may also have upset prices. An upset price usually applies when the property in question is in foreclosure, there is a trust deed, or their are liens. The outstanding debt is paid when the buyer purchases the property. In these cases, the property or merchandise cannot be legally "given away" for prices less than the debt against them. Usually, however, anywhere near the "upset" figure you've got a real steal.

U.S. Marshals Service:

See Marshals Service, U.S.

Viewing:

At the auction preview you are allowed to view, or look at and inspect, the items being auctioned. We strongly recommend you always take advantage of the auction previews and thoroughly check out the items you wish to bid on. This is especially important any time you wish to bid on a "big ticket" item. In Chapter 16 we give you suggestions on ways to determine the value of an item, along with tips on inspecting vehicles. The auction preview is really the only time you are allowed to do much viewing of an item. Also remember that at some places the auction is held at a different location than the auction preview.

"Where-Is":

This indicates that the buyer is responsible for moving any items he successfully bids on. The agency holding the auction will not deliver it for you. Before you bid on that airplane, car or yacht, make sure you have the means to haul it away. Most smaller items must be paid for and removed the day of the auction. In most cases you are allowed a specified number of days to remove larger items such as vehicles or heavy machinery.

AUCTION SUMMARY TABLE

AUCTION TYPE:	TYPES OF PROPERTY*:	PAGE NUMBERS:
BATF	V	166
BUREAU OF LAND MGMT.	RE	103,166-170
CITY POLICE	B,CAM,C,E,J,PP,S,V	17-19
COUNTY SHERIFF	A,C,E,J,O,PP,RE,V	37-45
CUSTOMS SERVICE, U.S.	A,B,C,E,J,LV,P,PP,RE,S,V	3,12,93,97-101,183
DEA - DRUG ENF. AGENCY	A,B,C,E,J,LV,P,PP,RE,S,V	3,53
DOA - DEPT OF AGRICULT.	C,O,V	175-176
DoD - DEPT OF DEFENSE	B,C,CAM,E,O,P,PP,V	3,121-133,183
DRMO / DRMS	B,C,CAM,E,O,P,PP,V	11,12,121-133
FDIC	A,C,E,J,O,PP,RE	171-175
GSA - GEN. SERV. ADMIN.	B,C,E,O,P,PP,RE,V	11,12,54,103-119,166,175,184
IRS - INT. REVENUE SERV.	A,B,C,E,J,LV,O,P,PP,RE,S,V	91-96,103,105
MARSHALS, CITY/COUNTY	A,C,CAM,E,J,LV,O,PP,S,V	37-45
MARSHALS SERVICE, U.S.	A,B,C,E,J,LV,O,P,PP,RE,S,V	1,53-63,104,186
POSTAL SERVICE, U.S.	C,J,O,PP,V	47-51
SBA - SM. BUSINESS ADMIN	C,E,J,O,PP,RE,S,V	135-146
STATE SURPLUS	B,C,CAM,E,LV,O,PP,V	65-89
TVA - TENN VALLEY AUTH.	C,E,O,PP,RE,V	165-166

*PROPERTY DESCRIPTIONS:
A = ANTIQUES, COLLECTIBLES, ARTWORK
B = BOATS, VESSELS
C = COMPUTER EQUIPMENT
CAM = CAMERAS, VIDEO EQUIPMENT
E = ELECTRONIC EQUIPMENT
J = JEWELRY, COINS
LV = LUXURY VEHICLES
P = PLANES, AIRCRAFT

PP = PERSONAL PROPERTY
RE = REAL ESTATE
S = STEREO EQUIPMENT
V = VEHICLES (CARS, TRUCKS, 4-WHEEL DRIVES, MOTOR-CYCLES, ETC.)

Businessman buys Maltese Falcon prop for $398,500

By ROB HAESELER and MARC SANDALOW
SAN FRANCISCO CHRONICLE

A rare Maltese Falcon movie prop was auctioned in New York for $398,500, far exceeding all estimates of its value and shattering the dream of two San Franciscans who wanted to fetch it home.

Christie's auctioneer Kathleen Guzman hammered down the icon to Ronald Winston, president of the New York-based Harry Winston jewelry chain. Winston outbid a field of more than 20 challengers, including San Franciscans John Konstin, owner of John's Grill, and his partner, veteran private investigator Jack Immendorf.

Konstin was on the auction floor in Manhattan connected by an open phone line to Immendorf at the grill in San Francisco as the bidding escalated. The whole thing was over in two minutes and 20 seconds.

"When it hit $110,000, I was scratching my head, deciding how much more to go," Immendorf said. "And then it was already $130,000 and then $140,000 and within 10 seconds it was over $200,000."

Glancing around the popular restaurant, the detective said: "Today, the main course is humble pie."

San Francisco was the setting for Dashiell Hammett's detective novel about hard-boiled private eye Sam Spade. Hammett, who worked as a Pinkerton man in the Flood Building on Market Street in the 1920s, frequented neighboring John's Grill and mentioned the historic restaurant in "The Maltese Falcon" as a place where Spade stopped to dine while searching for the elusive statuette.

Christie's was confident that the statuette would sell for more than the firm's original estimate of $30,000 to $50,000, "but our best internal guess was $150,000," Guzman said.

The Maltese Falcon, one of two known props created for the 1941 Warner Bros. classic of the same name starring Humphrey Bogart, was consigned to Christie's by the estate of William Conrad, the rotund television actor who died in Los Angeles in February.

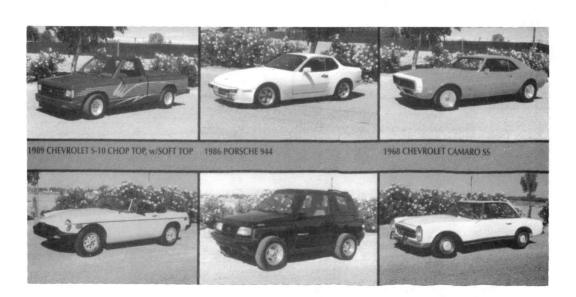

1989 CHEVROLET S-10 CHOP TOP, w/SOFT TOP   1986 PORSCHE 944   1968 CHEVROLET CAMARO SS

Figure 1:
Successful Bidders List

SUCCESSFUL BIDDER/ITEM SUMMARY LISTING   PAGE 19
FOR IFB 41-4581   25-August-
DRMO PORT HUENEME

BIDDERS	ITEM NOUN	QTY	PRICE
TOTAL			
0207 RICHARD	126 PRINTERS: 2 EACH.	1 LT	55.00
STC	234 TURN BUCKLES: EST 600 LBS.	1 LT	30.00
CLR MALIBU	239 RACKS, METAL: EST 2500 LBS.	1 LT	110.00
CA 90265	257 BUILDING MATERIAL: INCLUDING FLOOR	1 LT	150.00
	276 SEAVYS: 6 EACH.	1 LT	75.00
	363 CHAINS: EST. 850 LBS.	1 LT	40.00
TOTAL			460.00
0208 MARC	228 CABLE, ELECTRICAL: 2 REELS.	1 LT	75.00
STC	370 SCRAP, COPPER: EST. 760 LBS.	1 LT	600.00
CLR LOS ANGELES			
CA 90023			
TOTAL			675.00
0209 LOTTIE	232 TRANSMISSION: VEHICULAR.	1 EA	60.00
STC	275 AIR CONDITIONER UNITS: ENVIRONMENTAL,	1 LT	90.00
CLR PASALTADEN	281 PROPELLERS, SHIP: 3 EACH.	1 LT	75.00
CA 91001	366 PORTABLE BAR & DISPLAY CASES: 3 PCS.	1 LT	95.00
TOTAL			320.00
0212 JOE	191 RADIATOR & ENGINE PARTS: EST 300 LBS.	1 LT	25.00
STC	201 BUCKETS, AIR TANKS & ROTARY ENGINE	1 LT	55.00
CLR CARPENTERIA	204 VENTILATOR:	1 EA	10.00
CA 93014	205 PANEL, POWER DISTRIBUTION: CAROLINA	1 EA	160.00
	209 ENGINE WITH CONTAINER: 1976, WHITE	1 EA	150.00
	215 PUMPS, TRAILER ATTACHMENTS & HYDRAULIC	1 LT	75.00
	242 CABLE, ELECTRICAL: 5 REELS.	1 LT	325.00
	284 CABLE, ELECTRICAL: EST 900 LBS.	1 LT	200.00
	286 LANDING MATTING: PSP METAL, EST 1600	1 LT	230.00
	290 SCRAP, STEEL HEAVY, PREPARED: EST 2706	1 LT	600.00
	309 BEARING, O RINGS: 3 EACH, EST 30,000	1 LT	50.00
	328 FIRE HYDRANTS: 18 PCS.	1 LT	190.00

212

BI	BIDDERS	ITEM NOUN	QTY	PRICE
TO	TOTAL			272.5
01	0179 LEOPOLDO	166 SMOKE DETECTORS: 30 EACH.	1 LT	25.00
ST	STC	369 CHAIRS, LOUNGE: EST. 1200 LBS.	1 LT	12.50
CL	CLR OXNARD			
	CA 93030			
TO	TOTAL			37.5
01				
ST	018	218 TRANSMISSIONS: 3 EACH.	1 LT	200.00
CL	STC	219 COMBINATION TRANSFER UNITS: 2 EACH.	1 LT	230.00
	CLR GARDEN GROVE	253 TRUCK, TRACTOR: 5 TON, 6X6, MFG UNK,	1 EA	4900.00
	CA 92640	313 TRUCK, CARGO: 2 1/2 TON, YEAR UNKNOWN,	1 EA	4600.00
TO				
	TOTAL			9930.0
01				
ST	0181 CHARLES	198 HOSES: 3 EACH.	1 LT	10.00
CL	STC	292 TRAILER, WATER TANK: 1 1/2 TON, MFG	1 EA	800.00
	CLR SANTA MARGARITA	305 COMPRESSOR, AIR: 1964 GARDNER-DENVER	1 EA	375.00
	CA 93453	353 VEHICULAR COMPONENTS & ACCESSORIES:	1 LT	85.00
TO		356 FANS, MOTORS AND LIGHT FIXTURES: EST.	1 LT	110.00
01	TOTAL			1380.0
ST				
CL	0183 JOHN	274 AIR CONDITIONER UNITS: 1984,	1 LT	120.00
	STC	327 LAWN EQUIPMENT: 2 PCS.	1 LT	25.00
	CLR VENTURA	334 DIVIDERS, ROOM: EST 900 LBS.	1 LT	25.00
TO	CA 93001			
01	TOTAL			170.0
ST				
CL				
	0184 LLOYD	345 VISE, TABLE TYPE: 2 EA.	1 LT	65.00
	STC	350 PUMP, FUEL, TRAILER MOUNTED:	1 EA	260.00
TO	CLR LOS ANGELES	354 MAINTENANCE REPAIR SHOP EQUIPMENT: EST	1 LT	325.00
	CA 90001	362 CHAINS: EST. 400 LBS.	1 LT	30.00
02		364 CHAINS: EST. 700 LBS.	1 LT	110.00
ST				
CL	TOTAL			790.0
	0191 JOHN A	136 COVERS, VEHICLE: EST 300 LBS.	1 LT	260.00
	STC			
	CLR PHOENIX			
	AZ 85016			

Figure 2:
Notice of Award

ALL COMMUNICATIONS SHOULD INCLUDE THE CONTRACT NUMBER SHOWN IN BLOCK 5 BELOW

NOTICE OF AWARD, STATEMENT, AND RELEASE DOCUMENT

1. PAGE OF 1	

2. FROM: (Name and address of Sales Office)

LOCATION: DRMO PORT HUENEME BLDG BLDG. 513
NCBC PORT HUENEME

PORT HUENEME   CA 93043-4314

3. DATE OF AWARD — 14 September
4. INVITATION NO. — 41-4583
5. CONTRACT NO. — 41-4583-0018

6. TO: (Name and address of Purchaser)

7. BIDDER NO. — 0018
8. (PAID STAMP) Pd All 9/14/.. RH

PURCHASER WILL LOSE ALL RIGHT, TITLE, AND INTEREST IN THE PROPERTY WITHOUT FURTHER NOTICE IF NOT PAID FOR AND REMOVED BY 21-Sep
(For Release of Property Only)

NOTE: ONLY TIPS 3,4,5 & 8 ON REVERSE SIDE OF FORM APPLY TO THIS SALE.
This is to inform you that your firm has been awarded a contract of sale for the following materials as a result of the above numbered Invitation to Bid.

9. PROPERTY MUST BE REMOVED BY (Final date of removal) 21-Sep

10. SURPLUS AND/OR EXCHANGE/SALE ITEMS

ITEM NO.	DESCRIPTION	QUANTITY	UNIT	UNIT PRICE	TOTAL PRICE	QUANTITY RELEASED
80	COMMUNICATION EQUIPMENT: INCLUDING 1 - 194, BLDG 526, BAY	1	LT		75.00	1 LT
130	TYPEWRITERS, ELECTRIC: IBM, 8 EACH, 1 - 194, BLDG 526, BAY	1	LT		105.00	1 LT
154	OFFICE FURNITURE: INCLUDING CHAIRS, 1 - 194, BLDG 526, BAY	1	LT		40.00	1 LT
171	TYPEWRITERS, ELECTRIC: IBM, SELECTRIC 1 - 194, BLDG 526, BAY	1	LT		50.00	1 LT
178	ADP EQUIPMENT: EST 275 LBS. 1 - 194, BLDG 526, BAY	1	LT	XXXXX NOTHING FOLLOWS XXXXX	150.00	1 LT

11. RELEASE

An agent of the purchaser obtaining release of the material must present purchaser authorization.

A. I HAVE RECEIVED THE ABOVE LISTED MATERIALS IN THE QUANTITY INDICATED AND HAVE ACCEPTED SAME IN COMPLIANCE WITH THE TERMS OF ABOVE NUMBERED CONTRACT.

TYPED OR PRINTED NAME AND SIGNATURE OF PURCHASER OR AUTHORIZED AGENT

B. RELEASED BY (Signature)
C. DATE 9-15.   D. VOUCHER NO.
13. SALES CONTRACTING OFFICER (Typed or stamped name and signature)

12. STATEMENT OF ACCOUNT

Payment of amount due the U. S. Government must be made prior to removal of any material. Make checks payable to U. S. TREASURY.

A. TOTAL CONTRACT PRICE	$	420.00
B. LESS DEPOSIT	$	
C. BALANCE DUE	$	
D. REFUND DUE	$	
E. STORAGE CHARGES	$	
F. PAYMENT RECEIVED CASH	$	420
G. REFUND MADE	$	

DRMS Form 1427 Sep 85
(Previous editions to be used until exhausted.)

IMPORTANT NOTICE ON REVERSE

PART 1 – FOR OFFICE USE ONLY				
DATE	ITEM NO.	REMOVALS	PAYMENT RECEIVED ($)	REFUNDS MADE ($)

REMARKS

PART 2 – TIPS FOR PURCHASERS

You have been awarded the items listed on the reverse side of this document. In order to minimize confusion or any chance of you having to pay storage charges or your contract being terminated for failure to pay for and remove property, you should do the following:

1. If there is an amount due indicated in Block 12 C, you should remit this immediately to the sales office indicated in Block 2. **NO PROPERTY CAN BE REMOVED UNTIL PAID FOR.** Unless otherwise indicated in the IFB, MAKE CHECKS PAYABLE TO: U. S. TREASURY. Receipts are not furnished.

2. (Read Block 9). This is your final free removal date. If you do not remove the property by this date you will be placed in Default and storage charges will be assessed.

3. Make arrangement for pickup of property and send release authorizations to both the carrier and the disposal officer where the material is located. **THE GOVERNMENT WILL NOT ACT AS LIAISON IN ANY FASHION BETWEEN PURCHASER AND CARRIER.** If desired, a list of carriers serving the area is available from the Sales Office indicated on the reverse side.

4. Furnish your agent or carrier complete info needed to remove the property. **THE GOVERNMENT WILL ONLY MAKE INITIAL PLACEMENT WHERE IT IS PROVIDED THE GOVERNMENT LOADS. PLACING, HANDLING, PACKING, BRACING, BLOCK–ING, ETC., ARE YOUR RESPONSIBILITY**

5. If the IFB provided that purchaser loads, then you must make all arrangements for loading including any equipment you may require to accomplish such loading. **IN THESE INSTANCES, THE GOVERNMENT WILL PROVIDE NO ASSISTANCE.**

6. Follow up with your carrier or agent frequently, especially if you are in default. Extensions or reinstatements of your contract cannot be made because of your agent or carrier's failure to do something.

7. Upon receipt of property, inspect it immediately for misdescription. Misdescription claims filed after 30 days from date of removal will be denied as untimely filed.

8. If you have any questions regarding this award, contact the Sales Contracting Officer at once.

Figure 3:
DRMS Surplus Property Bidders Application

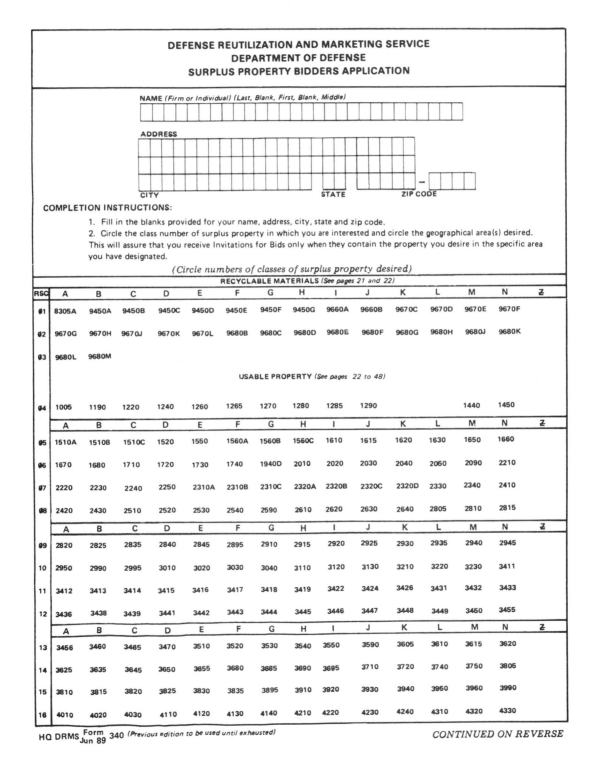

DEFENSE REUTILIZATION AND MARKETING SERVICE
DEPARTMENT OF DEFENSE
SURPLUS PROPERTY BIDDERS APPLICATION

NAME *(Firm or Individual) (Last, Blank, First, Blank, Middle)*

ADDRESS

CITY   STATE   ZIP CODE

COMPLETION INSTRUCTIONS:

1. Fill in the blanks provided for your name, address, city, state and zip code.
2. Circle the class number of surplus property in which you are interested and circle the geographical area(s) desired. This will assure that you receive Invitations for Bids only when they contain the property you desire in the specific area you have designated.

(Circle numbers of classes of surplus property desired)

RECYCLABLE MATERIALS *(See pages 21 and 22)*

RSC	A	B	C	D	E	F	G	H	I	J	K	L	M	N	Z
01	8305A	9450A	9450B	9450C	9450D	9450E	9450F	9450G	9660A	9660B	9670C	9670D	9670E	9670F	
02	9670G	9670H	9670J	9670K	9670L	9680B	9680C	9680D	9680E	9680F	9680G	9680H	9680J	9680K	
03	9680L	9680M													

USABLE PROPERTY *(See pages 22 to 48)*

RSC	A	B	C	D	E	F	G	H	I	J	K	L	M	N	Z
04	1005	1190	1220	1240	1260	1265	1270	1280	1285	1290			1440	1450	
05	1510A	1510B	1510C	1520	1550	1560A	1560B	1560C	1610	1615	1620	1630	1650	1660	
06	1670	1680	1710	1720	1730	1740	1940D	2010	2020	2030	2040	2050	2090	2210	
07	2220	2230	2240	2250	2310A	2310B	2310C	2320A	2320B	2320C	2320D	2330	2340	2410	
08	2420	2430	2510	2520	2530	2540	2590	2610	2620	2630	2640	2805	2810	2815	
09	2820	2825	2835	2840	2845	2895	2910	2915	2920	2925	2930	2935	2940	2945	
10	2950	2990	2995	3010	3020	3030	3040	3110	3120	3130	3210	3220	3230	3411	
11	3412	3413	3414	3415	3416	3417	3418	3419	3422	3424	3426	3431	3432	3433	
12	3436	3438	3439	3441	3442	3443	3444	3445	3446	3447	3448	3449	3450	3455	
13	3456	3460	3465	3470	3510	3520	3530	3540	3550	3590	3605	3610	3615	3620	
14	3625	3635	3645	3650	3655	3680	3685	3690	3695	3710	3720	3740	3750	3805	
15	3810	3815	3820	3825	3830	3835	3895	3910	3920	3930	3940	3950	3960	3990	
16	4010	4020	4030	4110	4120	4130	4140	4210	4220	4230	4240	4310	4320	4330	

HQ DRMS Form 340 Jun 89 *(Previous edition to be used until exhausted)*   *CONTINUED ON REVERSE*

RSC	A	B	C	D	E	F	G	H	I	J	K	L	M	N	Z
17	4410	4420	4430	4440	4450	4460	4510	4520	4530	4540	4610	4620	4630	4710	
18	4720	4730	4810	4820	4910	4920	4925	4930	4931	4933	4935	4940	4960	5110	
19	5120	5130	5133	5136	5140	5180	5210	5220	5280	5305	5306	5307	5310	5315	
20	5320	5325	5330	5340	5345	5350	5355	5410	5420	5430	5440	5445	5450	5510	
	A	B	C	D	E	F	G	H	I	J	K	L	M	N	Z
21	5610	5640	5650	5660	5670	5680	5805	5815	5820	5821	5825	5826	5830	5831	
22	5835	5840	5841	5845	5895	5905	5910	5915	5920	5925	5930	5935	5940	5945	
23	5950	5955	5960	5961	5965	5970	5975	5977	5985	5990	5995	5999	6105	6110	
24	6115	6120	6125	6130	6135	6140	6145	6150	6210	6220	6230	6240	6250	6320	
	A	B	C	D	E	F	G	H	I	J	K	L	M	N	Z
25	6340	6350	6505	6510	6515	6520	6525	6530	6540	6545	6605	6610	6615	6620	
26	6625	6630	6635	6636	6640	6645	6650	6655	6660	6665	6670	6675	6680	6685	
27	6695	6710	6720	6730	6740	6750	6760	6770	6780	6810	6830	6840	6850	6910	
28	6920	6930	6940	7105	7110	7125	7195	7210	7240	7290	7310	7320	7330	7360	
	A	B	C	D	E	F	G	H	I	J	K	L	M	N	Z
29	7360	7410	7420	7430	7440	7450	7460	7490	7510	7520	7530	7610	7710	7730	
30	7810	7830	7910	7930	8010	8030	8040	8105	8110	8115	8120	8125	8130	8135	
31	8140	8145	8305B	8340	8405	8410	8415	8420	8430	8435	8440	8445	8460	8465	
32	8475	8710	8820	9110	9130	9135	9140	9150	9160	9310	9320	9330	9340	9350	
	A	B	C	D	E	F	G	H	I	J	K	L	M	N	Z
33	9390	9505	9510	9515	9520	9525	9530	9535	9540	9545	9630	9640	9650		

STATES IN WHICH I AM INTERESTED (Circle the states desired)

34	01 - ALA	02 - ALASKA	03 - ARIZ	04 - ARK	05 - CAL(N)	52 - CAL(S)	06 - COLO
35	07 - CONN	08 - DEL	09 - DC	10 - FLA	11 - GA		13 - IDA
36	14 - ILL	15 - IND	16 - IOWA	17 - KAN	18 - KY	19 - LA	20 - ME
37	21 - MD	22 - MASS	23 - MICH	24 - MINN	25 - MISS	26 - MO	27 - MONT
38	28 - NEBR	29 - NEV	30 - NH	31 - NJ	32 - N MEX	33 - NY	34 - N CAR
39	35 - N DAK	36 - OHIO	37 - OKLA	38 - OREG	39 - PA	40 - RI	41 - S CAR
40	42 - S DAK	43 - TENN	44 - TEX(N)	53 - TEX(S)	45 - UTAH	46 - VT	47 - VA
41	48 - WASH	49 - W VA	50 - WISC	51 - WYO	54 - PUERTO RICO		55 - VIRGIN IS

CLASSES OF SURPLUS SHIPS, PONTOONS, AND FLOATING DOCKS IN WHICH I AM INTERESTED (Circle numbers of classes desired)

	A	B	C	D	E	F	G	H	I	J	K	L	M	N	Z
42	1905A	1905B	1905C	1905D	1905E	1905F	1910	1915	1925A	1925B	1925C	1925D	1930A	1930B	
43	1935	1940B	1940C	1945	1950	1990									

44	FOR ITEMS IN CLASSES 1905A THROUGH 1990 (EXCLUDING CLASS 1940D WHICH IS SELECTED BY STATE), CIRCLE ONLY THE GEOGRAPHICAL AREA(S) PROVIDED. 81 - EAST OF MISS RIVER (INCL GULF PORTS) 82 - WEST OF MISS RIVER 83 - OVERSEAS ONLY 84 - WORLD-WIDE

INDICATE ONE (Refer to How to Buy pamphlet, page 51)

☐ SMALL BUSINESS   ☐ LARGE BUSINESS

RETURN THIS APPLICATION TO THE FOLLOWING ADDRESS

DEFENSE REUTILIZATION AND MARKETING SERVICE
NATIONAL SALES OFFICE
PO BOX 5275 DDRC
2163 AIRWAYS BOULEVARD
MEMPHIS TN 38114-5210

Index

NOTES

NOTES

NOTES

NOTES